Understanding the Gyroplane

A Handbook of Technical Information for the Non-Technically-Minded

For Gyrocopters and Sport Autogyros

by Paul Bergen Abbott

All photographs and illustrations are by the author unless otherwise indicated.

Published by
The Abbott Company, Indianapolis, Indiana USA

Copyright © 1988, 1994 Paul Bergen Abbott
All rights reserved. No part of this book may be reproduced without permission.

Cristina—

May all your dreams take wing.

Contents

Chapter		Page
	Introduction	2
1	The Earliest Rotorcraft	6
2	The Gyroplane Finds Its Place in History	14
3	The Magic of Rotor Blades	22
4	What Makes the Blades Go Around?	28
5	Understanding Your Rotors	36
6	Regulations Affecting Gyroplanes	50
7	Licensed or Ultralight?	61
8	Aerodynamic Stability	69
9	Behind the Power Curve—What's That?	75
10	Beating PIO and Other Nasty Habits of the Gyroplane	81
11	Thin Air	105
12	Common Gyroplane Terms	116
	Index	120

The information in this book is provided for the enjoyment and education of its readers. It cannot be used as a basis for learning to fly, maintain or operate an aircraft. Those activities must be done with proper reference to appropriate technical manuals and with personal instruction by a competent person.

Introduction

Try to take off and fly without an aircraft. What happens? Your arms get tired. You sweat a lot. You don't budge from the ground.

A silly idea? Yes, but it's only slightly different from the idea of flying without a good, well-tuned gyroplane under you. And it's a whole lot like flying without a good understanding of how a gyroplane works.

Humans don't fly. Sure, we talk about it a lot, saying, "I can fly!" But we lie. It's our gyroplane that does the flying, not us. We sit on it and control it. We may build it or even design it, but we can't fly without it.

It doesn't matter how much we desire to fly, we still can't exceed the capabilities of our aircraft. And if that aircraft is underpowered or badly balanced or flapping its blades, we aren't going anywhere that resembles up.

That's why it's vitally important to understand the gyroplane on which we are totally dependent. If we can make it operate at its best—and if we ourselves can pilot it at our best—then we and our machine will achieve our greatest flying success.

This book will help you understand the gyroplane. It will explain how a gyroplane works and tell what makes a gyro fly successfully and unsuccessfully. It will give you technical knowledge explained in the kind of words you use every day.

Once you understand more about gyroplanes, you will probably be a better pilot. You will certainly be a more confident pilot, and you will be better able to figure out what happens when you fly.

Of course, you can fly quite well without understanding much about gyroplanes. If you have good instructions and follow them correctly, you can fly happily. You already do this with other devices. You already use complex machines without really understanding how they work. When you turn on your TV set to watch a ball game, who cares what all those integrated circuits are doing inside that set? When you take a picture of Rover with your Polaroid camera, who cares what chemical magic is transforming that blank square into a gleaming color picture?

When you take off in your gyroplane, who cares what those rotor blades are doing? Wait! That's a different matter! You do care. Even though your rotors will do their thing without your knowledge, your neck is at risk. If something unexpected happens you will feel far more comfortable if you understand it.

Even if you don't fly a gyroplane yourself, you'll probably find that the story behind these unique aircraft is fascinating. It's a tale of a magnificent obsession shared by some of the most inventive people in history. It's a study of the forces of nature set in balance and directed toward one result: picking you up and lifting you through the air on spinning wings.

You'll probably be surprised at how much is known about gyroplanes. Despite their brief and interrupted history these unique aircraft have been studied extensively. Before the first gyroplane flew more than 60 years ago, the inventor had to work out most of the basic principles of this machine. And what he didn't know at the start, he learned over the years, until the gyroplane was developed to a peak of efficiency and usefulness—over 40 years ago!

Today the emphasis of the rotorcraft world is not on gyroplanes but on helicopters, whose powered rotors make them operate differently from gyroplanes. Helicopters get all the attention and research dollars. But every one of those helicopters is designed to fly in autorotation, operating as a gyroplane in an engine-out emergency. That means a lot of effort and study (and big development bucks from the government) have gone into studying autorotation for helicopters. And just about all that knowledge can be applied to gyroplanes.

It would be a shame to miss out on all that good information. That's why I have gathered the most important ideas here in this book for you. I don't want you to miss out on understanding these fascinating machines we fly. Understanding gyroplanes is the goal of this book.

If, along with understanding, you want some information about piloting skills, I wrote another book for you. It's called "The Gyroplane Flight Manual". It's available from most of the same sources as the book you now hold in your hands.

There's a lot to know about gyroplanes. Some of it is in these books. Some of it is not. But the more you really understand, the more fascinating the whole subject becomes and the more you are able to function as if you were part of your gyroplane. And when you are part of your gyroplane, you come as close as possible to actually flying.

That's when you really can say, "I can fly!"

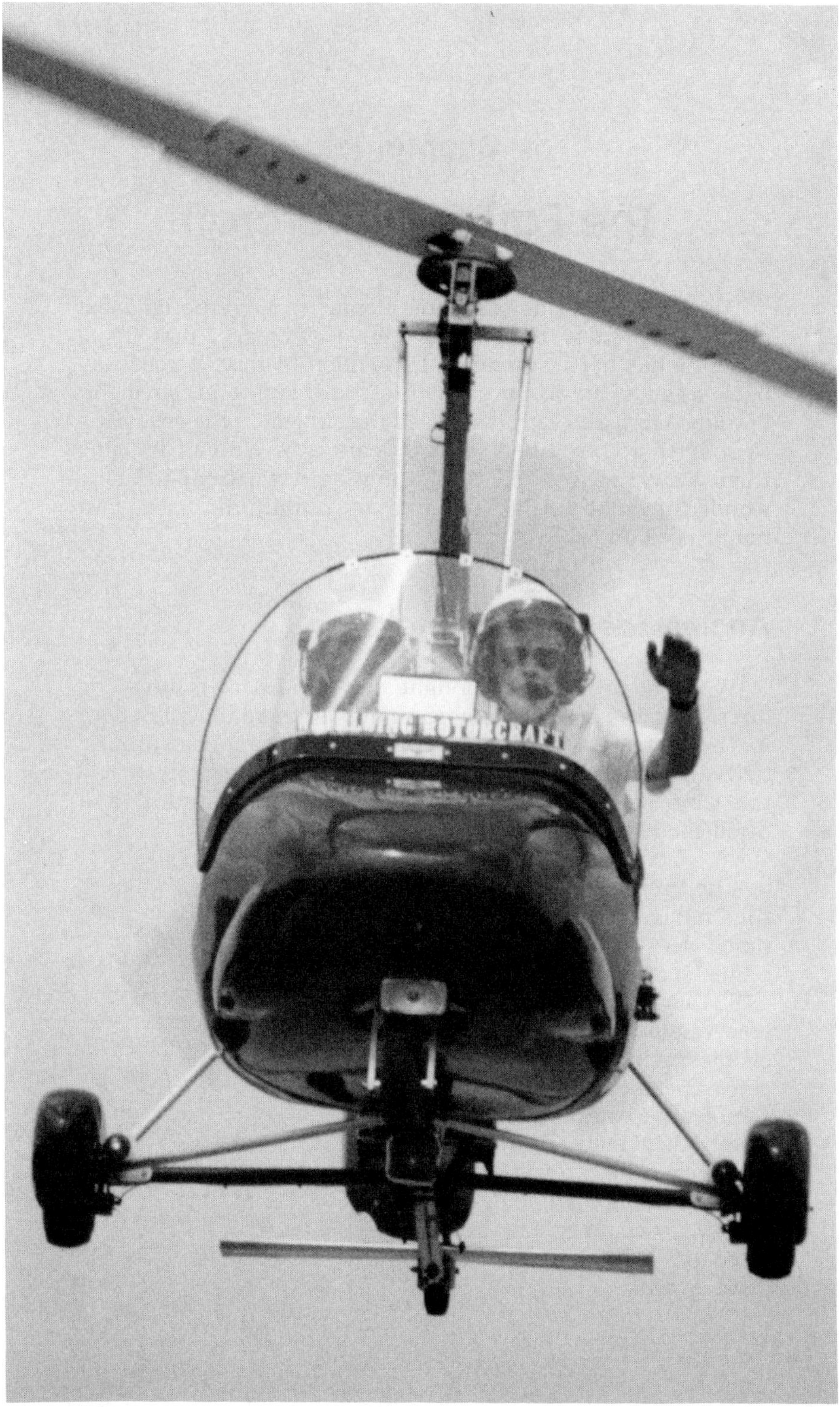
ROTORCRAFT

Chapter 1

The Earliest Rotorcraft

The gyroplane is not a new development. Even though most people alive today have never seen a gyroplane, that flying machine has been prominent in aviation history. It goes way back, as far as the obscure origins of the dream of human flight. Perhaps Morg and Ayla discussed the subject in the caves at a Neanderthal convention 50,000 years ago. We can imagine them watching a maple seed spinning down from the sky, wondering what would happen if you could jump on a giant maple seed and ride it.

Ancient ideas of rotorcraft

When someone first thought up the idea of rotory-wing aircraft, it was certainly before I could be there to write about it. The first important event we know about happened around 320 A.D., when the Chinese developed a toy rotorcraft we call the Chinese Top. It flew well, and was later studied and duplicated by some of the rotorcraft pioneers.

The first people who picked up the Chinese Top idea in more recent times were a couple of Frenchmen named Launoy and Bienvenu. In 1783 they built a small spring-powered version and flew it for a lot of people, including the French Academy of Sciences. It had a strong resemblence to the old Chinese toy but was made of feathers and driven by a tiny bow. The two Frenchmen considered scaling up their discovery to a size they could ride in, but recognized they didn't have a good enough power plant.

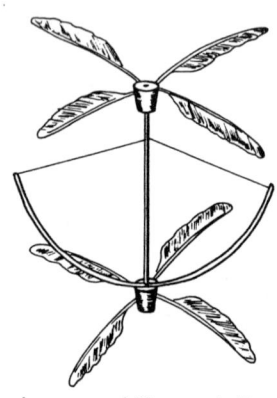

Launoy and Bienvenu's Top

Another version of the Chinese Top was built a few years later by an English schoolboy named George Caley, who was destined to become one of the famous idea generators in the history of aviation. Caley, too, dreamed of a larger machine he could fly in, and drew up plans in 1843. But without a suitable power plant the machine was never built.

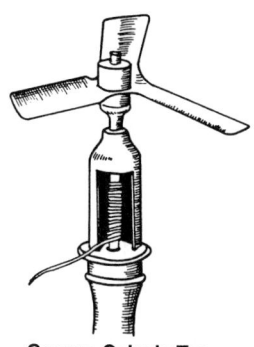

To avoid missing a person many people think was of importance to aviation, I'll mention Leonardo da Vinci. Actually, he was a much better painter than engineer, as you can tell from the rotorcraft he sketched in the 1480's. He also supposedly built models, but no one knows whether they ever flew. There's no evidence that da Vinci's work was ever considered by the people who eventually got rotorcraft to fly. He did coin a name for his machine that we can vaguely recognize, calling it his helixpteron, meaning "spiral wing".

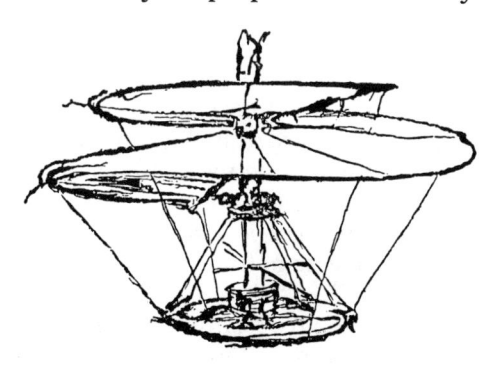

George Caley's Top

The first machines to carry the modern form of that name, "helicopter", were made in the 1860's by Viscount Gustave de Ponton d'Amecourt. They were tiny spring and steam powered rotorcraft.

Even the famous inventor, Thomas Edison, got rotorcraft fever for a while. In the 1880's Edison, fresh from inventing the phonograph and the light bulb, attempted to devise a "helicoptal aeroplane". But he gave up after failing to get enough power out of his engines that ran on electricity and explosives.

The first flying machine to be named "Gyroplane" was, in fact, a helicopter. In 1907 a Frenchman, Louis Charles Breguet, built the first rotorcraft to actually lift off the ground with a human aboard. Breguet called it his "Gyroplane No. 1". This may have been the source of the current name for the aircraft you and I are so fond of. Unfortunately, Breguet's machine was not controllable or capable of sustained flight, and was held in place by men holding on to all four corners.

Other inventors made attempts at building rotorcraft. Another Frenchman, Paul Cornu, hovered a 573-pound machine of just 24 horsepower in 1907. This gave Cornu the distinction of making the world's first free flight in a helicopter. Then a Russian named Igor Ivanovich Sikorsky (recognize that name?) made two unsuccessful attempts at building a helicopter in 1909 and 1910, but abandoned the effort and started building airplanes. Meanwhile other people built helicopters that rose off the ground: Jacob C. H. Ellehammer in Denmark in 1912, Emile Berliner in the United States around 1919 and George de Bothezat, whose 3600-pound helicopter lifted five men thirty feet into the air in the early 1920's.

Many other experimenters tried to achieve vertical flight, but the most promising rotorcraft were developed around 1922 to 1924. A Spaniard, Raul Pateras Pescara, flew almost half a mile. A Frenchman, Etienne Oehmichen flew more than a mile and stayed up almost a quarter of an hour. All these early attempts used some sort of power to turn some sort of rotor, so those early machines were actually helicopters, not gyroplanes.

Even the Wright brothers thought about rotorcraft in their early planning, before settling on a fixed-wing approach inspired by the hang gliders of Otto Lilienthal.

I suspect Wilbur Wright was wishing he had stuck with rotor blades instead of wings when he said, on approximately August 21, 1901, approximately these words: "If man ever flies, it will not be within our lifetime...not within a thousand years!" He was on his way back from some unsuccessful attempts at flight at Kitty Hawk, and (unkown to him) was only two years away from success.

As history and any gyro pilot will tell you, a real flying nut like Wilbur Wright would never quit trying until he succeeded. The Wrights made it on December 17, 1903 (with Orville aboard the first official flight, due to the luck of the draw).

Keep that date in mind, 1903, as you think about the next twenty years when airplanes went from the stick-and-fabric construction of the Wright Flyer to JN-4 Jennies and Sopwith biplanes of World War I. For twenty years it seemed like there was nothing but airplanes, airplanes, airplanes in the headlines and on everybody's mind. Even the people who were destined to be the pioneers of rotorcraft were busy building airplanes—people like Igor Sikorsky, Henrich Focke, Harold Pitcairn and a Spanish kid named Juan de la Cierva.

A Spanish kid dreams of flying

Juan, who lived near Madrid, developed a passion for airplanes while he was a teenager. In 1910 he and two of his buddies got together to build a glider they could fly off a hill by pulling a rope. They made successful low-level flights until Juan's little brother crashed from the unexpected height of 50 feet, getting knocked unconscious by the impact.

After such an experience, you'd think our old friend Juan would have had his fill of aviation. But did he quit and take up something calm like bullfighting? Did Wilbur Wright give up and go into dentistry? Is the Pope married? Are you kidding?!

Like the future gyro pilot he was, Juan de la Cierva pressed on. He and his gang of buddies bought a wrecked airplane, salvaging enough parts to build something they thought would fly. They painted it scarlet and called it the Red Crab.

Being just a bit smarter than your average teenager, Juan did not try to fly his airplane himself. Instead, he and his buddies got a Frenchman, Jean Mauvais, to act as test pilot for the occasion. Amazingly, this amateur-built creation flew well, until eventually the glue they had used went bad and the plane fell apart in a heap.

Cierva, who by now was getting older and wiser, continued to design airplanes. He built a large trimotor bomber with which he hoped to win the prize of 30,000 pesetas ($6,000) offered by the Spanish army. But on its second flight, the pilot got too slow in a low-altitude turn. The airplane stalled and crashed into the ground, destroying all hopes of prize money for Cierva.

The "impossible dream"

Cierva didn't get mad, he decided to get even. He then began his life-long quest to develop a safe aircraft, one that would be incapable of stalling or spinning. Imagine how ridiculous that idea must have seemed in 1920! At that time the only type of heavier-than-air flying machine that had ever flown successfully was the airplane. And everybody believed that stalls and spins were an unavoidable characteristic of flying machines.

It had taken decades of serious work to develop the airplane. That monumental task was accomplished by some of history's greatest inventors: Lilienthal, the Wrights, Curtiss—even Thomas Edison. Now, one audacious Spaniard proposed to single-handedly invent a second type of flying machine. Not even that famous Spanish legend, Don Quixote, would have dreamed this "impossible dream".

At this point it would be colorful but totally inaccurate to portray Juan de la Cierva as an obsessed, incredibly lucky character who was led to the solution by divine inspiration and incredible courage. Actually, the successful pioneers of flight were nothing like this. Cierva, like the Wright brothers, Otto Lilienthal and other successful developers followed a simple formula: Work hard; Test everything thoroughly; Fly the thing only when you can't find any other way to test it. The Wright brothers used a wind tunnel and lots of mathematics. They built airfoils, tested them, modified them, and did this over and over with a thoroughness today's engineers would respect.

Cierva took an orderly apprach, too. He conceived several different types of moving wings before he settled on the type you and I regard as the only way to do it. Think about it: Some of the moving wing ideas Cierva did not use may be technically feasible, and are still waiting to be developed by someone—maybe you!

Cierva tested various rotating wings in his wind tunnel and discovered how to make autorotation work. A patent on autorotation had already been granted to fellow Spaniard Raul Pateras Pescara, but his method used the negative blade angle of a windmill. Cierva discovered how to use a positive angle to produce the lift needed to fly.

Cierva experimented until he found the exact range of angles at which the rotor blades would be propelled horizontally. He built models of his proposed aircraft and test flew them until they worked so well there was nothing left to do but build a full scale, human-carrying aircraft. When he finally made his Cierva C.1, he had every reason to hope it would fly. It was a two-rotor machine with one rotor above the other. But interference between the two rotors threatened to topple the machine over when they tried to fly it.

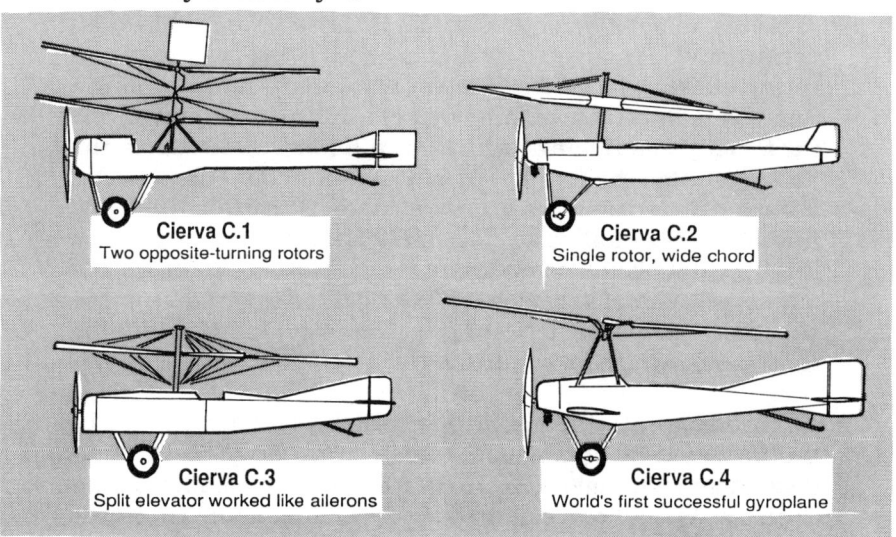

Cierva C.1
Two opposite-turning rotors

Cierva C.2
Single rotor, wide chord

Cierva C.3
Split elevator worked like ailerons

Cierva C.4
World's first successful gyroplane

Juan de la Cierva invented the gyroplane in only four tries.

Any aircraft builder can tell you that problems like that can really bug you! Cierva did his best to figure out what was causing the rolling problem, and decided that whatever the cause was, the solution was not in the double rotor. The bottom rotor was turning only two-thirds as fast as the top rotor, indicating its airflow was being partially blocked. He then built a machine with a single rotor of very wide chord blades, the C.2, but it had the same rolling problem. Cierva rebuilt this machine nine times before he went back to the drawing board.

His next machine, the C.3, used a single rotor which was braced with high-tensile steel wires. To try to overcome the rolling problem, it had an extra large elevator with split right and left sections that could be activated like ailerons. This machine hopped off the runway, but acted as though it wanted to turn over. On another flight it did capsize, registering history's first gyro rotor blade crunch. Cierva rebuilt this one four times.

A fateful night at the opera

When an aviation enthusiast runs into a problem like this, you know what happens: He thinks about it, night and day and in the oddest places. For Cierva, who was a member of the Spanish nobility, one of those odd places was the opera. While the fat lady was singing, Cierva was thinking. Suddenly, in the middle of Aida, he had it: His model gyros could fly perfectly because their rotor blades were made of rattan, which is flexible. But his full-scale gyros had rotors that were rigid. The flexible rotors could compensate for the unequal rotor speeds on the two sides of the machine. The rigid rotors couldn't, so the side that was moving forward produced more lift than the side that was moving backward, and the machine tried to roll over.

On January 9, 1923—in the twentieth year after the Wright brothers made their first flight—Juan de la Cierva's C.4 aircraft took off and flew, piloted by Army Lieutenant Alejandro Gomez Spencer. Its rotor was mounted by a flexible teetering hinge that allowed it to work just like the successful rattan models. Cierva had done it! He had invented a second type of aircraft, one that could not stall or spin!

Cierva named his invention the autogiro, claiming the word as his trademark. Only Cierva and his licensees could use that word. The rest had to change the spelling, using a 'y' instead of an 'i' to become "autogyro".

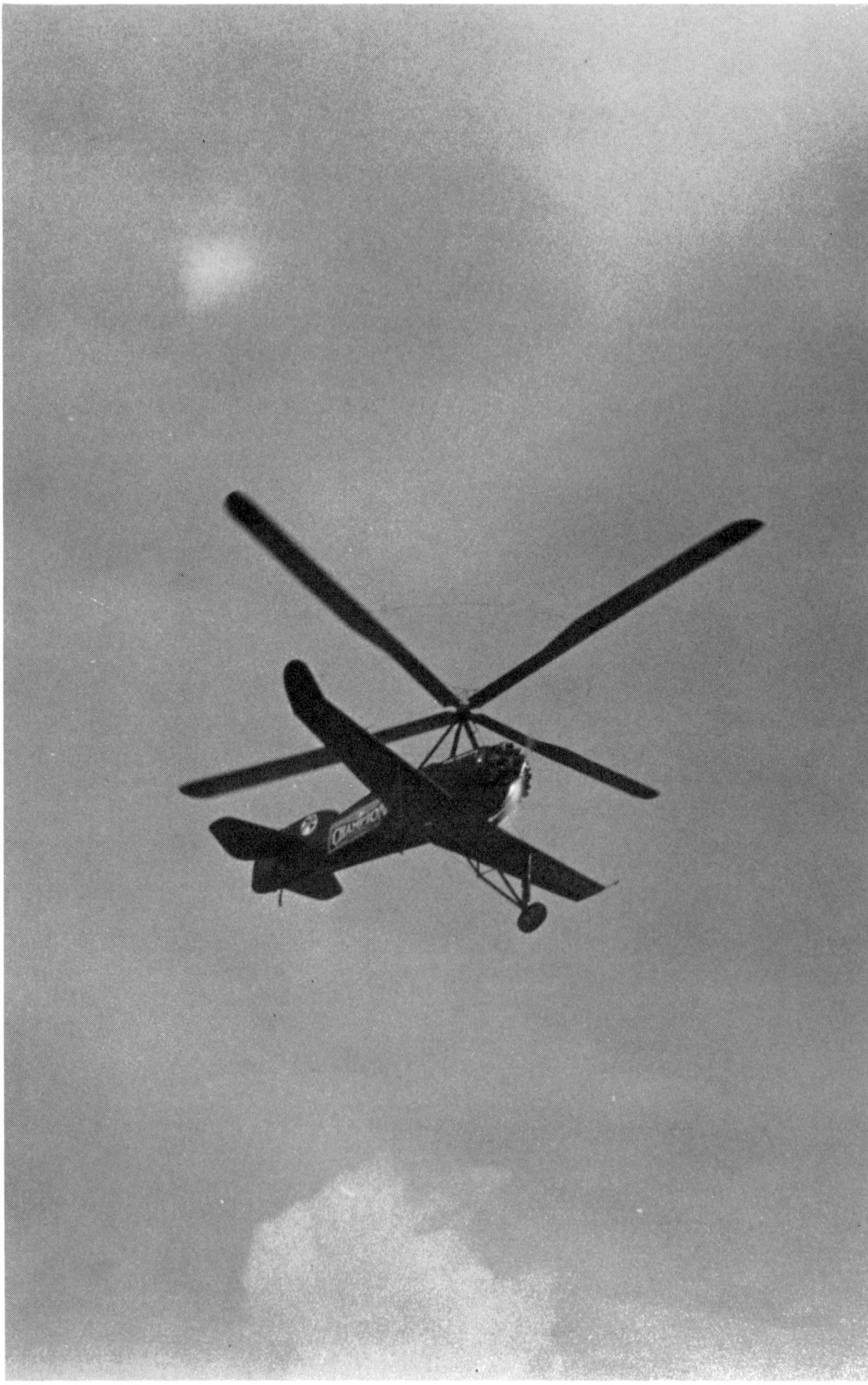

Chapter 2

The Gyroplane Finds its Place in History

The world's reaction to the autogiro eventually bordered on hysteria. In the years that followed its invention, Cierva's new type of aircraft became as hot as today's latest rock star, as newsworthy as the President's last news conference, as up to date as the Space Program.

The autogiro was featured in the most prominent media of the day: magazines, newspapers and the Roaries Twenties equivalent of TV, the newsreels. An autogiro starred in a first-run movie. One of these aircraft landed on the lawn of the White House, to the delight of President Herbert Hoover and Orville Wright, among other dignitaries. Then it took off and flew away over the horizon.

Autogiros were flown by the top names in aviation, like Charles Lindbergh, Amelia Earhart and Jimmy Doolittle. These were the same type of aircraft we fly today called gyroplanes. They looked different, with the engine in the front and an airplane-like fuselage. The rotors turned slowly, only a little over 100 rpm, and at first the rotor heads did not tilt. These early gyros were controlled by small wings with large ailerons and airplane-like tail surfaces.

Cierva and Pitcairn lead the way

Cierva quickly developed and refined his machine, working from his factory in England. He was helped and often rivaled by a noted American airplane builder, Harold Pitcairn, who dropped everything to devote his efforts to developing autogiros in the United States. Pitcairn developed the first engine-powered prerotator on his 1931 PCA-2 autogiro. Pitcairn and

Ciervia both came up with a jump takeoff device, in which the rotors, temporarily set at 0° pitch, were spun much faster than flying speed. A lever was thrown which clicked the blades into positive pitch and transferred all engine power to forward thrust. As a result, the gyro jumped vertically into the air and began to fly forward. It was spectacular!

Cierva and Pitcairn each developed autogiros with tilting rotor heads, so that the wings could be removed and the autogiros became pure rotorcraft. This made a big difference in performance, and the autogiros of the late 1930's and early 1940's rivaled the performance of the best airplanes of the day. It can be argued that Cierva and Pitcairn made the greatest gyroplanes or autogyros in history. To give you an idea, consider the 1939 PA-36 Whirlwing. This all-metal gyro had a closed cabin with room for two people aboard. To demonstrate it, Pitcairn circled it tightly with cars. It then did a 30-foot-high jump takeoff, flew around the field and landed right back in the circle.

Another U.S. manufacturer, Kellett, made a series of autogiros under license from Cierva. One of these used to make regular mail runs, doing takeoffs and landings from the roof of a post office in Philadelphia.

Perhaps Cierva and Pitcairn did too good a job, making it seem as though they could do anything with the autogiro. Eventually people added a new request: "Make it hover!" Soon that request became a demand.

Unfortunately, the hovering machine came along, but from the worst possible source: that old enemy from World War I, who was becoming more and more a rival each day—Germany! In 1936 Henrich Focke demonstrated the world's first operational helicopter, the Focke-Achgelis F.61. It had twin counter rotating rotors, one mounted on each side of the aircraft. In 1938 the Germans flaunted their new toy with daily demonstrations flying inside a building!

That made the Americans, the British and all the other rivals of Germany green with envy. The pressure to build a helicopter became overwhelming. The answer to the Germans came in 1938 when our old friend, Igor Sikorsky, now living in the United States, made his first shaky attempts to take off in his VS-300 helicopter. By 1939, it was flying.

Sikorsky's machine had a single main rotor and a tail rotor to offset torque, much like most of today's helicopters. Sikorsky's machine was good, but alas, contrary to popular belief, it was not the first helicopter. The helicopter could not have been invented so soon without the earlier invention of the autogiro, which we now call a gyroplane. Both Sikorsky and Focke learned about rotorcraft from Cierva and the autogiro world.

What happened to the autogiro?

Why didn't the autogiro continue to be developed on its own? Some say that it was no longer needed once the helicopter was invented. Some say the demands of World War II distracted the aviation community toward building Mustangs and Thunderbolts. Some say it was the sudden loss of the champion of the autogiro. Juan de la Cierva died in the crash of an airplane taking off in a London fog in 1936. Development of his machine was soon dropped by his company, and Pitcairn's company eventually shut down. Pitcairn himself was eventually involved in developing a helicopter, the XR-9, which reportedly outperformed previous Sikorsky models. Then Pitcairn, like Cierva, met an early death, in a handgun accident.

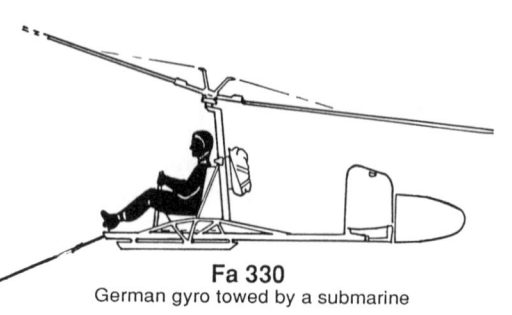

During the war an obscure new aircraft was developed, destined to have a strong influence on you and me. The Germans built a light open-frame rotorcraft without an engine, the Focke-Achgelis Fa 330. This three-bladed gyro was towed by a cable high above German submarines, while the pilot reported what he saw by telephone. When trouble was spotted, the craft was reeled in, folded up and stowed inside the submerging U-boat.

Fa 330
German gyro towed by a submarine

The British had their own version of this concept. Theirs was also a very small open-frame rotorcraft without an engine, but was intended to be towed behind an airplane. Called a Rotachute, one of these craft found its way to the General Electric Company after the war. There the Rotachute was evaluated by a team under the direction of a young engineer named Igor B. Bensen.

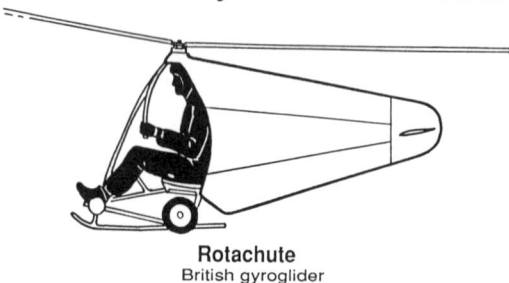

Rotachute
British gyroglider

The Bensen Gyrocopter

Bensen had piloted several of the earlier autogiros. As a participant in the era of great popularity of the autogiro, he believed in the future of these rotorcraft. He left G.E. and formed his own company in 1953, beginning development of an aircraft of his own. After building several machines, Bensen finally settled on an aircraft that vaguely resembled a Rotachute with an engine added behind the pilot. It had a two-bladed wooden rotor, a simple airframe bolted together of round aluminum tubing, and was powered by a 42-horsepower Nelson engine.

This machine, the B-7, was completed in 1955 and trademarked the Gyrocopter. While this first Bensen gyro was beginning to attract public attention, Bensen was searching for a power plant with more oomph than the little Nelson engine. Eventually he found it, the McCulloch engine, a 72-horsepower two-stroker with 100 cubic inches of displacement. Best of all, these engines were cheap and plentiful in those days, since they were left over from Air Force use in target drone aircraft.

The McCulloch engine produced enough power for a bigger, stouter machine. Bensen introduced his model B-8 in 1957, made with two-inch square aluminum tubing, a wooden rudder, an overhead control stick and a steel spindle-type rotor head. This machine, with refinements, is the famous Gyrocopter which Bensen Aircraft Corporation produced for the next 30 years. It became one of the most famous sport aircraft and was at one time the most popular homebuilt aircraft in existence, beating out the Variezes, the Pitts Specials, the Thorp T-18's and the other well-known designs.

The Bensen Gyrocopter got a dual reputation in the early years. On one hand, there were a handful of enthusiasts who flew Gyrocopters and considered them to be an excellent, airworthy aircraft. On the other hand was almost everybody else. It seemed to many people that the Gyrocopter was strange (because it certainly didn't look like a Piper Cub) and that it was dangerous (because it looked odd, because learning to fly it was difficult and risky and because a lot of people were hurt and killed in these machines that they didn't understand). A lot of people thought Gyrocopters didn't really fly (because there were so few of them and pilot proficiency was generally not great).

Some airport operators objected to Gyrocopters in the early days, treating them as though they were not "real" aircraft and keeping them off their airfields. For a while many people questioned the sanity of anyone who would fly a Gyrocopter, but also envied the magnificent flying freedom gyro flyers obviously experienced.

While Bensen and his staff worked to improve the Gyrocopter, innovations for it were being developed everywhere, and many of these were adopted by Bensen. Lots of components changed, but the basic Gyrocopter remained the same. Here are some of the changes:

- The McCulloch engine eventually could be souped up to 90 horsepower;
- The more manageable offset gimbal rotor head was developed;
- An optional joystick was added to more closely match the aviation standard;
- Metal and composite rotor blades replaced the original wooden ones;
- A combination seat and fuel tank did away with the old "flying lawn chair" look.

The Bensen Gyrocopter was an important influence on the development of amateur-built aircraft. It focused attention on low-cost, easy-to-build aircraft. It was a focal point for sport rotorcraft enthusiasts, serving as the basis for establishing the Popular Rotorcraft Association, the organization of sport rotorcraft enthusiasts.

The Gyrocopter served as the platform for launching other rotorcraft developers, like Ken Brock, Dennis Fetters, Bill Parsons, B. J. Schramm and others. Each of these developers first flew a Gyrocopter before developing his own significant aircraft. Bensen's machine also influenced modern factory gyroplanes, including the Air and Space 18A (designed by Ray Umbaugh, a Gyrocopter veteran), the McCulloch (Javonovich) J-2 and a recent new gyro, the Hawk (Groen brothers). All of these abandoned the engine-first style of the original autogiros and used the Bensen-style pusher configuration.

For a while it seemed as though the Bensen Gyrocopter was the only sport rotorcraft in existence. But other experimenters were quietly at work in those early days of the 1950's. One of the most notable was Arliss Riggs, a self-taught developer of a long line of front-engine gyros. While he never sold or promoted his machines, he produced a series of highly original designs, reportedly ranging in quality from not-so-good to excellent. Other early experimenters included Jerrie Barnett and Chuck Vanek, whose quiet efforts have been more widely recognized in recent years. In England, Commander Wallis developed a highly successful line of small gyroplanes.

The modern era

The most recent development in sport rotorcraft came in the mid-1980's, when the ultralight movement lured thousands of new people into gyros. New engines became available for this expanding market and new gyro designs were introduced to use them. An explosion of manufacturing activity began, and continues today.

Ultralight rotorcraft erased the barrier of federal licensing and allowed new people to jump quickly into gyros without having to build them. While that may sound like a formula for disaster, another development helped push the rotorcraft movement toward its greatest success to date: The development of two-seat powered trainers and gyro flight training centers made flying lessons in a gyroplane as accessible as in an airplane.

Today the image of gyroplanes and their pilots has changed completely. Gyros are now recognized as a mainstream part of sport aviation. They are widely accepted at airports. Many airport operators, who used to drive them away, now openly seek gyros to come fly at their airfields. The safety of gyroplane flying has improved, and while there are still accidents, they are better understood by the public.

Today the gyroplane has earned its place as an important aviation vehicle. Over the years it has served in many roles, from commercial aircraft to movie star. Looking back at all that has happened since Juan de la Cierva gave the world his heroic invention, we can be sure that the development of the gyroplane is not over.

Chapter 3

The Magic of Rotor Blades

What one thing sets rotorcraft enthusiasts apart from airplane drivers, balloon riders and your average man on the street? Answer: rotor blades!

That pair of planks twirling above your head turns an engine and a pile of hardware into a flying machine. They mysteriously make 500 pounds or more of material and occupant become lighter than air. When rotor blades pick up enough speed to change from visible solid objects to an invisible blur, they do wondrous things—and we usually take them for granted.

But sit back, my friend, for we are about to give rotor blades the attention they have been missing. We are about to recognize some of the wonderful things they do. And we are about to find out that they do these things as if by magic.

Of course there's a scientific explanation for everything rotor blades do. For example, autorotation can be explained by drawing vectors that show that lift has a forward component which exerts a propulsive force on the blade. But that kind of explanation seems to take some of the wonder away from the amazing way rotor blades work. And it's not really necessary to understand all of that to be a gyroplane pilot. So for now we're going to ignore the vector drawings and the scientific explanations. First let's admire the apparent magic performed by these amazing rotor blades.

You see, hardly anybody actually puts gauges and meters on a spinning rotor blade to measure all those vectors you would study in a scientific approach. Nobody has actually felt that forward component of lift that supposedly pulls the blades around against the wind. The scientific theories about rotor blades have been carefully worked out and measured as well as possible. And they are considered to be proven by a simple fact: they work. But understanding the scientific explanations isn't nearly so important as understanding the almost magical things they do.

For example, once you start them, rotor blades will autorotate up to their normal speed and then, all by themselves, maintain that speed plus or minus no more than ten percent, no matter how fast or slowly you fly. The speed of the rotors on a gyroplane is so dependable that no tachometer is required by the FAA to indicate rotor rpm's.

Also, gyroplane rotor blades will automatically give you more lift when you need it! To illustrate, imagine putting a 50-pound sandbag on your lap and flying around in your gyro. Your rotor blades will actually speed up to help you carry that sand bag! Or, even without the sand bag, if you pull a sharp bank or flare for a landing, the rotors speed up to produce the extra lift you need.

It's amazing that a rotor blade that's only about seven inches wide can do the work of an airplane wing seven times that width. A rotor blade does it simply by spinning around, reaching about 350 miles per hour or so at the tip. And when it does, that flimsy, floppy rotor blade that drooped when it stood still suddenly becomes stiff enough to lift you and your machine clear off the ground—without any wing struts or cantilevered spars to prop it up!

Rotor blades are stiffened by something that used to be called *centrifugal force*. When you spin an object around in a circular path, there appears to be a pull toward the outside of the circle. In the case of rotor blades, that pull is quite strong, enough to make those blades more rigid, in effect, than if they were made of steel! While that pull was called centrifugal force for centuries, it now is called by a new name, centripetal reaction. But the effect is the same. In a rotor blade, it allows the blade to be small and light, but stiff enough to hold you up securely.

Now, to examine another seemingly magical action of rotor blades, imagine that you are pulling a 60-degree bank in a gyro, while the guy right next to you is doing the same thing in an airplane. The textbook says that the guy in the airplane will be pulling about two G's in a 60-degree bank.

But not you. Not while you're hanging from your rotor blades. As if by magic, they spill air through the spinning disc so that you always pull something closer to one G. This is good, since extreme maneuvers never feel as uncomfortable in a gyroplane as they do in an airplane. But it's bad, since that more comfortable feeling can tempt you to do a little fancier flying in the gyro than you should.

Gyroplane rotor blades do all these things so well, without any help from the pilot, that they seem to have a mind of their own. Here's a list of what we've mentioned so far: 1) They automatically maintain the proper rpm's, 2) They automatically give you more or less lift as you need it, 3) They automatically stiffen themselves, and 4) They automatically spill air to keep closer to a one G load.

Rotor blades will also, without any help from you, automatically change their angle of attack as they move from the advancing to the retreating side. This was one of the discoveries made by Juan de la Cierva that made rotorcraft possible. When Cierva was working on inventing the first gyroplane, at first he fastened down the rotor blades solidly like a propeller. He did that on the first three machines he built. These machines with their rigid rotors took a lunge at turning over on their sides, sometimes with disastrous results.

To solve the problem, Cierva invented a device called a flapping hinge that allows the rotor to do its own magical adjustment of angle of attack. This was a simple solution to a very difficult problem.

The problem is that as the gyroplane moves forward, its rotor blades are moving at different speeds through the air. For example, let's assume a gyroplane is flying along at 50 miles per hour. At the same time the rotor blades are spinning at, say 300 miles per hour at the tip. On one side (usually the right side in the United States) one of the rotor blades is moving forward—the advancing blade. On the opposite side (usually the left side in the United States) the other rotor blade is moving backward. This means that the advancing blade is actually moving through the air at 350 mph (300 mph for the blade plus the 50 mph speed of the gyro) while the retreating blade is moving through the air at 250 mph (300 mph for the blade minus the 50 mph speed of the gyro).

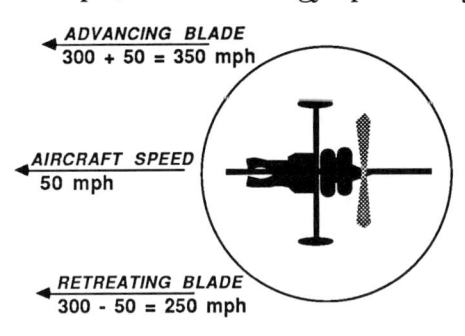

ADVANCING BLADE
300 + 50 = 350 mph

AIRCRAFT SPEED
50 mph

RETREATING BLADE
300 - 50 = 250 mph

With one rotor blade moving through the air at 350 mph and the other moving at 250 mph, something has got to give. You'll have more lift on the 350 mph side and less on the 250 mph side, and the machine will try to roll over. That's just what happened to Cierva's first three gyros.

This is just the sort of problem you should take to the opera, according to Cierva. There he figured that by simply allowing the rotor to pivot at the center (at the teeter bolt), the rotor blades would automatically correct for the unequal lift. The advancing blade would tilt down, reducing the angle of attack and creating less lift, while the retreating blade would tilt up, increasing the angle of attack and generating more lift. They do this each time they spin around, every second you are flying, and they do it all by themselves, as if by magic!

Yes, we'll get to the scientific explanations, in the next chapter. And if you like, you'll be able to study the vector diagrams and draw them on the back of napkins to amaze your friends. But when you're up there in the air, just you and your gyro, you won't need the diagrams. Your rotor blades will be performing their amazing dance several hundred times a minute, without any script or formula. They'll keep on spinning, flapping, advancing, retreating, and adjusting everything for themselves. It happens so fast and so perfectly that you will probably agree—it seems like magic!

Maybe that's what makes rotorcrafters so special. Maybe it's because they get to spend their Saturday afternoons so close to something so magical as rotor blades!

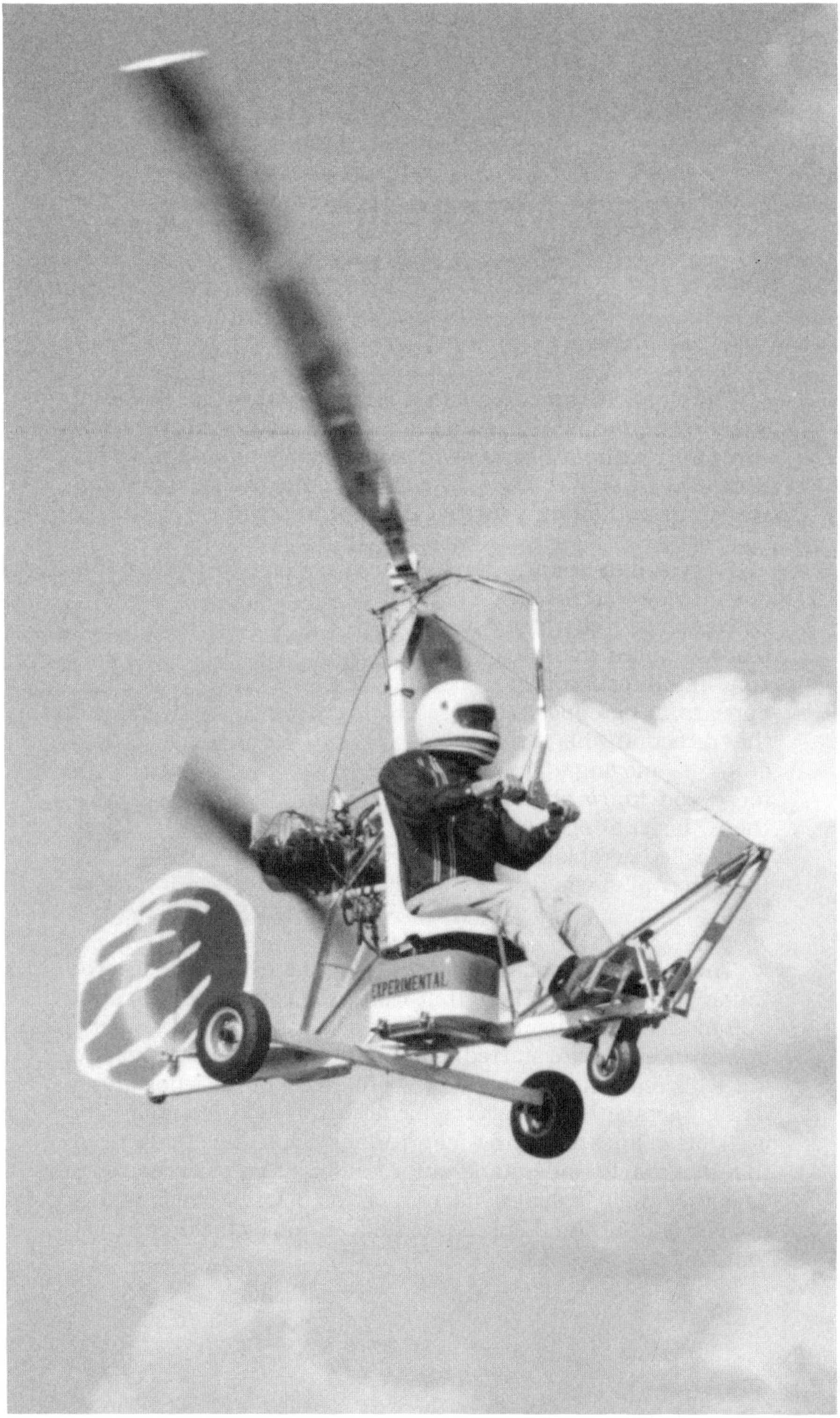
EXPERIMENTAL

Chapter 4

What Makes the Blades Go Around?

The simplest way to explain what causes the rotor blades of a gyroplane to spin is to call it magic and forget it. You can fly very nicely without ever knowing much about how rotor blades work. They will automatically spin up to the proper rpm's and stay there without any further thought from you.

But you may be curious to know why the air flowing past the rotor blades causes them to spin in a direction that appears to be opposite the direction the aircraft is moving. The more you know about these fascinating aircraft called gyroplanes, the better pilot you will be.

The spinning of rotor blades on a gyroplane is called "autorotation". As you can tell by that word, the rotors seem to spin automatically by themselves, never needing any direct engine power once they are started. This ought to be simple to explain, since it's really not a complicated process. But the whole thing usually gets rather messy. It typically involves a vector diagram with lots of lines and arrows. Fortunately, you don't really need that diagram to understand autorotation, as you will soon see. Of course, we'll look at a diagram or two before we're finished, but you should find them easy to understand by the time we get to them.

Helicopter Rotors versus Gyroplane Rotors

One good way to understand the autorotation of gyroplane rotors is to contrast them with helicopter rotors. They both look pretty much the same in flight, but they are actually working in opposite ways. On a gyroplane the air is flowing *up* through the disc formed by the spinning rotors. On a helicopter the air is flowing *down* through the rotor disc.

Air won't just naturally flow down through rotors. It takes an engine to make that happen. The job of a helicopter engine is to spin those rotor blades with enough force to grab those umptillions of air molecules above the rotors and smash them down towards the earth. Those umptillions of sub-microscopic collisions are what holds the helicopter up. They produce what we commonly call "lift".

It's commonly believed that air goes the opposite direction through gyroplane rotors—up through the rotor disc. Some of it does, slipping between the blades and through the center of the disc. But the air that's involved in producing lift actually moves down from the rotor blades. The rotors sneak up on air molecules on the underside of the rotor, smash them on the head and send them spinning out the back. Those umptillions of molecular collisions add up to lift, just as on a helicopter.

Airflow through gyro rotors

The Adventures of Mike The Air Molecule

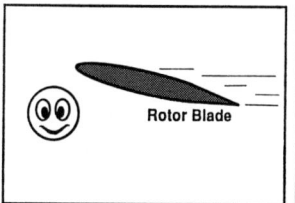

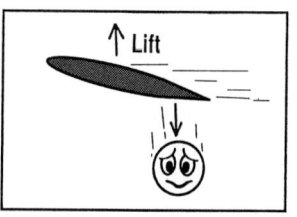

In both the helicopter and gyroplane the collision between air molecules and rotor blades accelerates the molecules toward the ground. And, as Isaac Newton told us in his Third Law of Motion, "For every action, there is a reaction, which is equal in force and opposite in direction." This means that if you smash enough air molecules toward the ground to add up to a combined force of 500 pounds going downward, that's how much lift you'll have pushing upward, holding up the aircraft.

So rotor blades produce lift by colliding with countless air molecules, accelerating the molecules downward and resulting in lift that pushes upward.

In a helicopter the air molecules end up on the bottom side of the rotors after this collision. In a gyroplane they end up on the top side of the rotor. That's mainly because the helicopter rotor is generally tilted forward while the gyroplane rotor is generally tilted back. The air flow follows a similar path past both aircraft, but there's a difference between the two: The gyroplane rotors are powered in autorotation by all those molecular collisions. When gyroplane rotors are hit from the bottom, the rotor is pushed around. But when helicopter rotors are hit from the top the rotor is slowed down, and they require an engine to keep them moving.

That's why a helicopter with an engine failure must quickly disconnect the engine and tilt the rotors back for autorotation. The pilot of a helicopter has a few seconds to convert his helicopter into a gyroplane or his rotors will slow down too much to keep working.

Autorotation

Now you're ready for the explanation you came to hear: What makes the rotor blades turn in autorotation?

To answer that question in a very simple way, we'll look at a couple of concepts. These are two mental pictures that will allow you to visualize what is happening when those blades go around.

There's nothing wrong with keeping things simple. And there's definitely nothing wrong with turning the idea of autorotation into a mental picture. This is the approach used by the great thinker, Albert Einstein. To come up with his Theory of Relativity, Einstein spent many, many hours concentrating, trying to imagine what happens to matter when it moves at the speed of light. When he finally developed a mental picture (a "concept") of what was going on, he really understood it. It was only after he had this understanding that he wrote down the famous formula that expresses the idea: $E = mc^2$.

As far as I can tell, it's a whole lot easier to get the mental picture of autorotation than to visualize the Theory of Relativity. With just two mental pictures we can go a long way toward making you an Einstein of gyroplanes.

The "Skipping Stone" Concept

Did you ever skip a stone across the top of the water? If you use the right-shaped stone, and if you throw it just right, it can collide with the surface of the water in such a way that it bounces back up.

Let's think about what happens with that stone. To skip properly, you used a reasonably flat stone, right? And you threw it in such a way as to hit the surface of the water at a very shallow angle, with the front end up. Then the stone bounced up. If you accidentally let it hit with the front end down it dug into the water and immediately submerged.

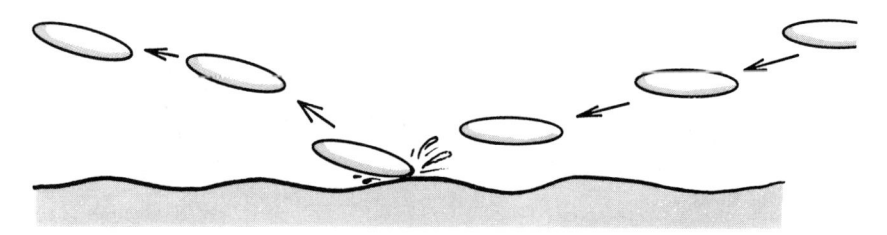

Now compare what happens to skipping stones with what happens to rotor blades. When the rotors are tilted back, as they are in a gyroplane, they are hitting the air molecules at an angle about like a skipping stone. The result of that collision is that the rotors "bounce" off those molecules and are pushed in an upward, forward direction. That push is mainly upward, giving you lift. But it's also slightly forward, and that's enough to spin the blades.

The "Skipping Stone" Concept makes it all so simple. Rotor blades autorotate the way a stone skips off the water. With this in mind, it doesn't seem so complicated.

At this point we could confuse things by jumping to the engineer's drawing and by describing force vectors. But before we put on our engineer hats, let's refine our skipping stone image by adding another nice simple idea that will help you get a mental picture of what your rotor blades are doing.

The "Squirting Soap" Concept

To have the complete picture of autorotation, I'm going to draw you one more picture. You see, the skipping stone image allows you to see the blades skimming along over the onrushing air, pushing upward to generate lift. But you may not quite see how this push is directed slightly *forward*, in addition to being upward.

To get a feel for the forward movement, imagine a bar of soap, preferably a nice used one that's very wet and sort of oval shaped. In your mind, take that wet bar of soap in your hand and, holding it between your thumb and fingers, squeeze it.

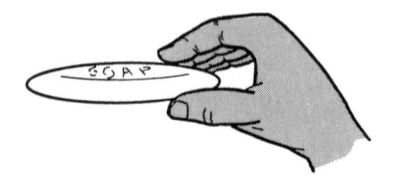

What happened? To no one's surprise, the bar of soap squirted out from your hand, maybe even sailing clear across the room. When you do it right, you can really get some speed and distance out of that squirting soap.

32

The reason that soap squirts is: 1) It's slick, and 2) You are holding on to a triangular-shaped object that has to move forward to allow your thumb and fingers to come together. When you squeeze, you put pressure on that triangle and it moves forward. It won't move any other direction. It won't move sideways. It won't move backward. But it will move forward, and with a good bit of speed.

Suppose that, instead of a bar of soap, you are holding on to a rotor blade that is triangular shaped. Suppose it is very slick and you are holding it between your thumb and fingers like the bar of soap. Now squeeze hard. Zip! The rotor blade squirts forward just as the soap did.

Take a look at the diagram below, showing the infamous vectors that we've been talking about with a bar of soap and fingers superimposed over it. You can see that the forces operating on the rotor blades squeeze it along the dotted lines just the way your fingers squeeze a bar of soap. The oncoming air applies the same pressure as your thumb. Pressure from the other side comes from the forward motion of the rotor blade. The result is a triangular-shaped situation just like the bar of soap. And the result is the same. The blade must move forward. It can't relieve the pressure by going backwards, sideways or up or down. It can only relieve the pressure by moving forward.

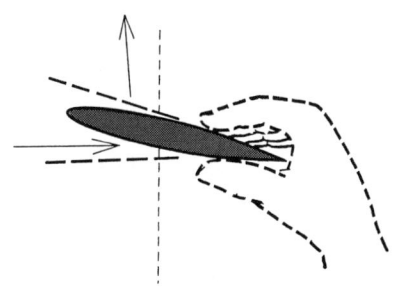

If you take away the drawing of the soap and hand, the vector diagram becomes mysterious again. The rotor blade isn't actually shaped like the bar of soap. In fact, a blade that's perfectly flat will autorotate. But the forces still work in a triangular fashion. The push of the air comes against the bottom of the blade at an angle. This makes up one side of the triangle. The momentum of the spinning blade resists this push and is, in effect, the other side of a triangle.

If you were an engineer, you would simply say that the lift which is generated has a forward component. While that makes sense, you may be able to understand autorotation better by thinking of it as a constant pinch of a bar of soap, which causes the blade to move forward.

This is a mental picture that will help you really understand what makes those blades go around. They are constantly bouncing off the air like a stone skipping off the surface of the water, producing lift. All the while they are constantly being pinched like a bar of soap, causing them to rotate foward, apparently against the oncoming wind.

This action is continuous, never ceasing while the machine is in the air. It's not magic, after all, but a result of very simple forces—like the ones that make a stone skip off the water and a bar of soap squirt from your hand. These are very dependable forces, as dependable as those that hold you up when you walk along the ground. And after a brief exposure to them in the seat of a gyroplane, you learn to trust them completely, just as you trust the earth to support you when you walk.

Now let's take an engineer's-eye view of the vector diagram. This is actually just a drawing of the spinning rotor blade from a side view, but I've drawn in the air flow and the direction of the forces acting on the blade. To make it easier to see, I've exaggerated the angles a bit.

There's an engineering principle that says the direction of lift is always perpendicular to the direction of the airflow meeting the airfoil. So if you draw a right angle going up from the airflow in front of the blade, you end up with an arrow that is tilted slightly forward. That forward tilt is the forward component of lift, and that's what makes the blades go around.

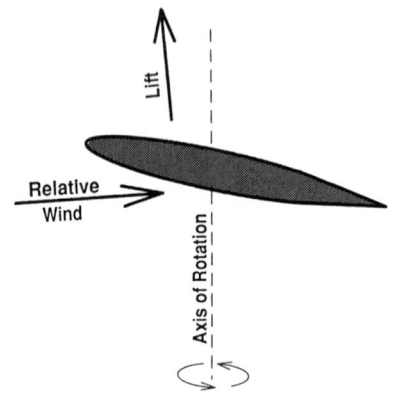

34

Notice that the momentum of the spinning blade presses against the oncoming air to prevent the blade from backing up. It's as if the blade were locked in position. That momentum is an enormously strong force when the blade is spinning at flying speed, and there's no way for the oncoming air to overpower it. But at slow speeds, as when starting your rotors, the momentum is weak and the blades can move up away from the airflow. When that happens we call it flapping.

The momentum of the spinning blade is a necessary part of the package of forces required for blades to autorotate. Autorotation is only possible if the blades are already spinning. In a way, it's a bit like a gasoline engine, which can run if you spin it, but which can't do anything from a standing start. The momentum of the blade is part of the triangle of forces that pinches the blade like a bar of soap and makes it keep rotationg.

Why are rotor blades hard to start?

Rotor blades are hard to start simply because they always run in high gear. It's like trying to get a stopped car moving when it's already in overdrive. The engine will struggle and cough, barely able to get the car rolling. As the car picks up speed, the engine, already in high gear, does a better and better job of moving the car. Finally, when the car is on the highway going at high speeds, the engine is easily able to move the car along in high gear.

Rotor blades have one gear ratio. It's like the bar of soap, where the soap must move several inches to allow the fingers and thumb to move only a half inch or so. The rotor blades must move seven or eight inches to allow air molecules to move together less than an inch. That's about an 8:1 gear ratio—definitely more like a high gear than a low gear. That's why rotor blades don't seem to pick up speed very quickly at first.

When started by hand, the blades seem to take agonizingly long to pick up those first few rpm's. But the faster they spin, the faster their speed increases. And, when finally near flying speed, rotor blades pick up speed very rapidly and maintain that speed very easily, just as the car in overdrive has no difficulty maintaining cruising speed on the highway.

Chapter 5

Understanding Your Rotors

Think of the greatest dancer you ever heard of—Fred Astaire, Mikhail Baryshnikov, even Gypsy Rose Lee. Not one of those fleetfoots could come close to matching the incredible dance performed by the rotor blades of a gyroplane! No human could ever wiggle, shimmy and bounce the way your rotor blades do, tirelessly, hundreds of times per minute.

If rotor blades look like a set of wing-shaped slabs that just spin around and screw you upward into the air, then you're missing an exciting story. What's really going on in that invisible cone formed by your whirling rotors is an aerial ballet without equal.

To enjoy the Bolshoi, you don't have to know how ballerinas stand up on their toes without falling over. And to fly a gyroplane well, you don't have to know the details of the pas de deux performed by a pair of rotor blades. But it's a fascinating story which, as you read on, you will hear.

How Rotor Blades Move

Rotor blades don't just spin. Besides going around, they also have to handle two different kinds of movement: 1) Rotor blades **teeter**, moving up and down, and 2) They deal with **lead and lag** forces that push them forward and backward. If they didn't have these actions, you wouldn't be able to fly your gyroplane.

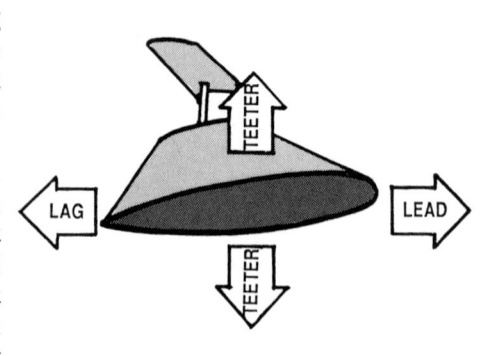

This was discovered the hard way by the inventor of the gyroplane, Juan de la Cierva. After a lot of experimentation, he got his rotor blades to autorotate just fine on his very first full-size gyro. But he had to build and re-build his machines thirteen more times before he made his rotors teeter, and he had to endure a frightening crash before he made his rotors lead and lag.

Teetering

Let's look first at teetering, the up and down movement of rotors. This is the primary way a set of gyroplane rotors overcomes the unequal speeds of the blades on the two sides of the aircraft.

On one side (the right side for rotors that spin in the standard direction for the United States), the rotor blades are moving forward. This is the *advancing* side. On the other side the rotor blades are moving backward. This is the *retreating* side.

Naturally, since the whole aircraft is moving forward, the right blade will tend to produce more lift than the left blade. This is called *dissymmetry of lift*.

Our hero Cierva recognized right at the start that this would be a problem. He tried several methods of overcoming dissymmetry of lift, starting with two rotors mounted one above the other, turning in opposite directions. That didn't work, so he tried a mechanical arrangement that was supposed to change the pitch of the rotor blades as they spun around, giving the advancing blade less pitch and the retreating blade more pitch. He couldn't get that to work, either.

It turned out that the simplest solution worked best. Cierva attached each rotor blade with a hinge that allowed it to wiggle freely up and down. As a result, the advancing blade had less pitch while the retreating blade had more pitch. The blades automatically equalized the lift on the two sides of the aircraft.

Advancing Blade

Relative Airflow →

Angle of Attack

Retreating Blade

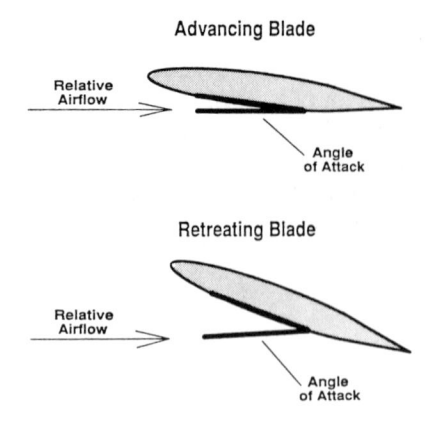

Relative Airflow →

Angle of Attack

Angles are exaggerated to make the difference easier to see.

Your gyroplane does this, and it does it even more simply than Cierva's machines. Your sport gyroplane probably has two rotor blades, mounted very simply on a single bolt in the center. Unlike Cierva's four-bladed rotors, your two blades just teeter in a see-saw fashion. When one blade teeters up, the opposite blade teeters down.

Your two-bladed rotor also makes teetering easier to understand. You can see it in the diagram on the opposite page, in which we've made a two-bladed rotor out of a flat piece of material. Since it's mounted on a teeter bolt in the center, it actually forms a universal joint (sometimes called a Hooke's joint). That way the rotor can spin in a circle that's independent of the shaft on which it's mounted.

But notice what happens to the pitch of the rotors. On the near side, the rotor blade is pointed down compared to the circle in which it is rotating. On the opposite side it is pointed up. There's negative pitch on the near side, positive pitch on the far side.

That's how your two-bladed rotor adjusts its pitch on the two sides of your machine. Unlike this flat bladed rotor, your rotor has positive pitch. So on the advancing side (the near side) it has less pitch and on the retreating side (the far side) it has more pitch.

I like the term "teetering" for this action. It is often called "flapping" or "feathering" by helicopter engineers. In gyroplanes, the word flapping often is considered a bad word, describing an excessive rotor movement on a botched takeoff, when the machine is taxiing too fast for the rotor speed.

Retreating Side

Positive pitch

Negative pitch

Advancing Side

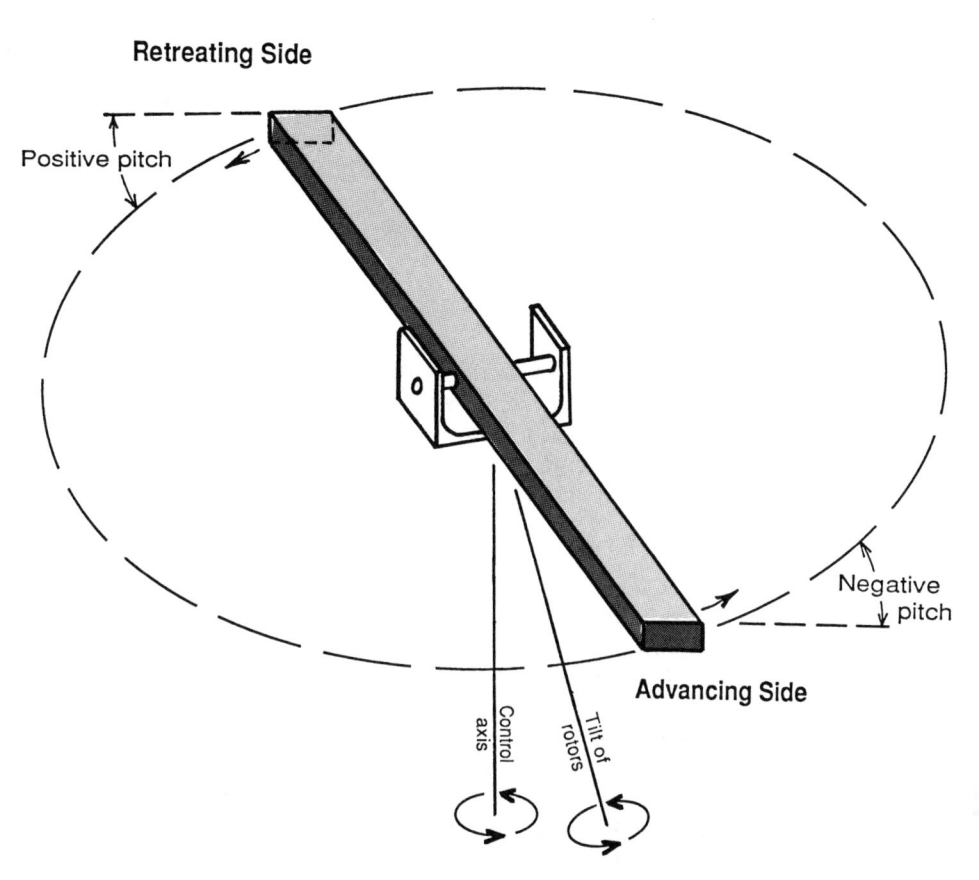

Control axis

Tilt of rotors

Your rotor blades teeter like this about ten times per second. They do it automatically without any help from you. If they were to stop teetering, your gyro would have a tendency to roll toward the retreating side (That's the left in the U.S.). This has been experienced by a gyro operating in very dirty conditions where dust and grit was allowed to build up on the teeter bolt and restrict its free movement. The machine tended to roll to the left, requiring the pilot to hold constant pressure on the stick, making it difficult to control. This rolling tendency was easily eliminated by cleaning the teeter bolt and its mountings.

Nearly all sport gyroplanes use a "semi rigid" rotor, made up of two blades mounted on a teeter bolt without any hinges. This is the simplest arrangement possible, and it's hard to beat for small gyros. If you were to complicate things with three or more rotor blades, you would need a teetering hinge at the base of each rotor blade. (Rotorcraft designers typically call this a "flapping hinge".)

Lead/Lag

This is not an important action with the two-bladed rotors commonly used on sport gyroplanes. These rotors are designed to minimize lead/lag action. However, it is good for you to understand the forces that cause a rotor to lead and lag because they are potentially destructive in rotors with more than two blades.

That's what Cierva found out in 1925. Unfortunately, the father of rotorcraft didn't listen to his test pilot, Frank Courtney, who was suggesting that the rotors should be hinged so that each blade could move forward and back. One day, at about 1,000 feet, Courtney heard a groaning sound from the rotor. He immediately began to descend, with the machine shaking alarmingly. Before it reached the ground, two of the four rotor blades had broken completely off and the gyro was smashed. (Courtney was hurt but survived. But he immediately resigned as Cierva's test pilot.)

Cierva found that the rotor blades had broken in fatigue at the roots. He determined that this was due to lead/lag forces which the rotor could not absorb. The test pilot was right. The problem was solved by putting a second set of hinges (commonly called drag hinges) at the base of each rotor blade to allow them to lead and lag.

Your semi-rigid rotor doesn't have drag hinges. The popular two-bladed rotors do not permit the blades to lead and lag independently as they spin. Some lead/lag movement is permitted by the resiliency of the blades and of the mast, which can flex a little. But most of the lead/lag force is controlled by the rigidity of the blades, and the fact that the lead/lag tendency is mainly cancelled out by two blades running in opposite positions.

There are several causes of lead/lag forces acting on gyroplane blades:

Universal joint effect

If you had a rotor with more than two blades the universal joint effect would cause your rotors to lead and lag. This is because a rotor sometimes moves as if it were rotating on two different shafts. A universal joint is not a constant velocity joint; When one side of a U-joint is driven at a constant speed, the other side rotates in a series of accelerations and decelerations. Your rotor blades would do that, too. But since you have a two-bladed rotor, the blades do not have to lead and lag individually from universal joint effect.

Coriolis Force

If two rotor blades track exactly opposite each other, you have no lead/lag tendency from coriolis force. But slower and multi-bladed rotors have a big problem caused by having to independently bounce off countless little updrafts and downdrafts as they go around. These put coriolis force on the blades.

To illustrate, think of an ice skater starting a spin with her arms and legs held out from her body. Her speed of rotation is reasonably slow. But for a big finish she pulls her arms and legs in and rotates at increasing speed into a blur. With arms out she spins slowly. With arms in she spins faster. This is due to coriolis force.

Like the skater pulling in her arms, a rotor blade spins faster if it flexes up. You can see that in this illustration, showing a pair of rotor blades running exactly opposite each other. The diameter of this rotor is shown by the dotted line between A and B. In the next illustration the right blade has bounced up from a gust or updraft (The amount of deflection is exaggerated to make it easier to see). Now the right blade is temporarily moving as if the rotor diameter were smaller, the distance between C and D. That means coriolis force makes it move faster, so it moves forward more than the other blade. It leads. By the same method, if a blade were to flex down it would temporarily have a larger diameter and would lag.

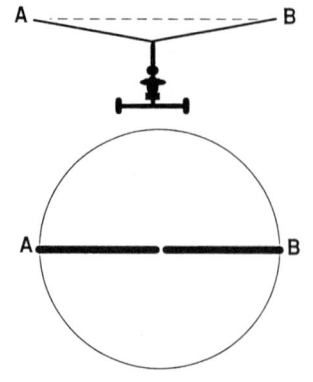

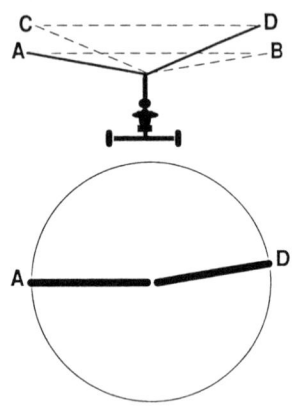

Other lead/lag forces

There are other forces pushing multi-bladed rotors to lead and lag. There are periodic changes in drag as the blades switch from the advancing side to the retreating side and vice versa. Fortunately, all these are easily handled by modern two-bladed semi-rigid rotors.

Types of Rotors

Semi-rigid rotors - Your sport gyroplane rotors use a wonderfully simple solution to a complex problem, the semi-rigid rotor. Your rotor has two rotor blades mounted rigidly to a hub that pivots on a teeter bolt. There are no flapping hinges or drag hinges.

Articulated rotors - Another type of rotor is the one originally invented by Cierva for his autogiros, sometimes called the "Cierva rotor". An articulated rotor is attached to the hub with flapping hinges and drag hinges, and has drag dampers. This is the most common tupe of rotor on helicopters.

Rigid rotors - This is a fairly recent development, used on just a few helicopters. A rigid rotor does not allow the blades to pivot freely at the hub. Instead they are held solidly in place. To overcome the unequal forces on the rotor, other provisions have to be made, including pre-coning and feathering of the blades.

> **Pre-coning** is done with common sport gyroplane semi-rigid rotors as well as with the helicopter rigid rotors. The blades are mounted to the hub at a pre-set coning angle so that they are angled slightly upward, with the tips higher than the roots.
>
> **Feathering** requires a very fancy mechanism, and is used on rigid rotors. Since the blades can't teeter, they have a device that actually twists each blade to adjust the pitch as it goes around. The advancing blade automatically twists to a lower pitch setting. Then, when it becomes the retreating blade it twists to a higher pitch setting. As you can imagine, this gets to be a very complicated device.

Tracking and Balancing Rotor Blades

You can fly perfectly well without knowing about the aerial ballet performed by your rotor blades as they teeter and lead and lag. You can also probably fly just fine without ever tracking or balancing your blades. That's because rotor blades can now be purchased which are ready to use. They are matched to each other, precisely balanced, and made to track closely together.

You should also know that there are hazards involved in tracking your rotor blades. ***Tracking is an extremely dangerous activity.*** Some of the methods involve standing close to rotors spinning as fast as you can get them to go. ***If those spinning rotor blades hit any part of you, that part will be instantly removed, whether it is a hand, an arm or a head!*** For that reason, tracking should only be done by the very careful and dedicated few who understand this high risk and are willing to accept it. I will not be responsible for what happens to you if you attempt to track your blades.

Tracking

It is desirable for each rotor blade to track exactly in the path of the previous blade. If both the blades follow exactly the same path, the rotor will run smoothly and be more efficient. If one blade runs high and another runs low, they will shake once per revolution (one per rev).

No two blades are exactly identical, no matter how perfectly they are intended to duplicate each other. They can be made to track closely, but typically some variation in the paths of the two blades is present. A small amount of out-of-track condition is no problem, causing nothing more than a little one-per-rev shake of the control stick.

You may be able to see variations in tracking at the airport if you're close enough and at just the right angle to see the blade tips of a machine that has stopped on the ground with its blades turning rapidly. Sometimes you can see an inch or more of space between the blur of each blade tip. That's enough to be felt by the pilot in the control stick, though a lot of them routinely fly that way and have come to accept that stick shake as a normal condition.

Methods of Tracking

There are several methods of rotor blade tracking that have been used successfully. Several of these involve parking the gyro, then spinning up the rotor as fast as possible with a pre-rotator. As an alternative to using a pre-rotator the machine could be taxied to bring the blades up to speed, but this involves the increased risk of someone rushing up to the rapidly spinning blades to measure them before they slow down.

Trial and error tracking - This is the safest, most widely used tracking method for sport gyroplanes. It's safer than the other methods because no one has to get near the spinning rotor blades. It's widely used because it's simple and one person can do it unassisted.

The first step is to take off and fly the gyro, feeling for a one-per-rev shake in the control stick and looking at the tips of the blades to see if one blade tip appears to be running lower than the other.

If you see and feel an out of track condition, there's no way to know which blade is riding low. So with the machine parked and the engine and rotor blades stopped, pick a blade and give it a slight positive pitch (This assumes that there is some means of adjustment, such as an adjustable hub or trim tab.) . Then secure the blade. (One of the risks of this method is the possibility of forgetting to tighten the mounting bolts and to secure them with pins or safety wire after you've made a trial adjustment.)

On your next hop, try to determine whether the change helped or hurt. It there's less shake, adjust the same blade to more positive pitch until it runs smoothly. If there's more shake, set that blade back to its original pitch and try putting a little positive pitch into the other one.

It's good to write down what adjustments you've made so that you can eventually get your blades to run very smoothly and in track.

Flag tracking - Each rotor blade is marked at the tip with a different colored chalk or crayon. The rotor is spun as fast as possible and a flag is moved toward the blades until it touches the tips and marks are made on the flag.

By comparing the space between the two colors, the amount of tracking difference is seen. Then, after the rotor has stopped, the blade that is tracking low can be increased in pitch or the blades tracking high can be decreased in pitch until they make identical marks on successive trials.

The flag is best made of canvas or stout fabric and should be securely attached to a pole which is held with its base against the ground. This ground contact prevents any up and down movement of the flag by the person holding it, who will undoubtedly be frightened and nervous standing so close to those potentially lethal blade tips!

Flag tracking using a pre-rotator. Note that the flagman crouches low to avoid those potentially lethal spinning blades. The flag rests against the ground.

Two blades strikes show up on the flag, indicating a slight out-of-track condition. One shows the red color of the chalk on the tip of one blade, the other mark is blue.

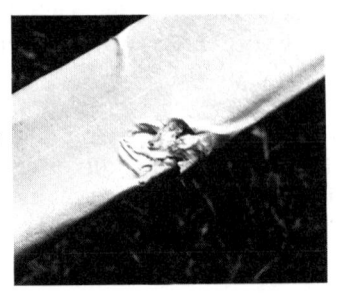

Brush tracking - Instead of a flag, this method uses a brush with long bristles mounted on a long pole. The brush is dipped in oil, removable paint or some other material that will leave an observable mark on the rotor blade. With the blades spinning at maximum speed, the brush is moved up gradually from underneath the rotor until it makes contact. When the rotor is stopped, the blade with the mark is shown to be tracking low.

The rotors are stopped and adjustments are made until successive trials produce a mark on both blades. The pole holding the brush does not have to be held against the ground, but caution is necessary to make sure the person holding the brush is standing clear, since it is held under those spinning rotors.

Light marker tracking - A source of light is attached to the blade tips, with each tip marked by a different color. These could be mirrors ("cats eyes") which reflect light from a lamp, or they could be small electric light bulbs or perhaps even some of those electroluminescent strips they sell at Disneyland. By spinning the rotors in at least partial darkness, the difference in tip path can be observed from a safe distance. This method could be used with the machine in flight, with an observer on the ground checking it carefully.

Stroboscopic tracking - An identifying mark is placed on each blade tip. Then, in reduced light, the blades are spun and observed in the light of a stroboscopic tachometer (a "Strobotac"). This is essentially a rapidly repeating camera flash unit (like the ones at discos, only faster). It can be adjusted to synchronize with the speed of the rotors. In the strobe light the rotors appear to stop, and the space between them can be seen clearly. This can be done at a safe distance from those infernally dangerous rotor blade tips! For helicopters, this method has also been used in flight, with the strobe light shining from the cockpit.

Electronic tracking - This has been used on helicopters, with electronic sensors reading the tip paths of the blades in flight. Some fancy new systems even adjust the pitch of each blade while the helicopter is flying! Small electronic units that are usable on homebuilt rotorcraft are now becoming available.

Balancing

Rotor blades need to be balanced very precisely, since even a slight out-of-balance condition will be magnified by the enormous inertial energy in spinning rotors. Out-of-balance rotors produce a one-per-rev shake much like out-of-track rotors.

Fortunately, ordinary balancing is not dangerous at all. It can be done in your garage, hallway or even your family room to the accompaniment of your favorite TV re-runs. All you need is a place where the air is motionless and you have room to hang your assembled rotors on their teeter bolt.

The teeter bolt should be placed on something that allows it to pivot freely. (I made a little stand that utilizes ball-bearing slot car wheels.) It is possible to balance your rotors while they are mounted on your machine. To do so you must make sure the teeter bolt is level and that the machine is propped up so the blades are free to move to a level position.

If your blades balance, the hub will be perfectly level. But you'll find that even a slight variation in weight, like a penny placed on the tip of one blade, will cause them to tilt noticeably. If your blades need adjustment (They probably won't), do it according to the manufacturer's recommendations, either adding or removing weight. (Before you correct an apparent out of balance condition, make sure you are not fouling up an even more precise dynamic balance that may have been done by the manufacturer, as described below.)

We've just talked about *static balancing*, which is accomplished while the blades are motionless. There's also an even more precise method, *dynamic balancing*, in which the blades are checked while they are spinning. This requires special electronic equipment that is not generally available, and is used by some blade manufacturers.

Dynamic balancing accounts for differences that only show up when the blades are spinning. To illustrate, if one of your blades were heavy at the tip and the other were heavy at the hub, you'd have a problem. If you did a static balance and then flew the blades, you'd find them shaking as if they were out of balance. In fact, they would be. When they spin, the blade that is heavy at the tip will have more outward pull than the blade that is heavy at the hub.

Rotor blades are made in as nearly identical pairs as possible, but even microscopic differences in consistency can affect their balance when they spin at 400 rpm or so. That's where dynamic balancing pays off, adding that last measure of smoothness to the rotors.

You may have dealt with balancing the wheels of a car. You probably found that you can get along okay with the "bubble" balance, which is a static balance. But for ultimate smoothness you need a "spin" balance, which is a dynamic balance. It's too bad the boys down at the tire store don't do rotor blades!

Chapter 6

Regulations Affecting Gyroplanes

They say you can't avoid death and taxes and, if you fly, the FAA. If you take off and fly around in any kind of an aircraft in the United States, you are regulated in what you do by the Federal Aviation Administration. (Of course, if you fly in another country you actually can avoid the FAA, but you will probably be under local rules that are also quite restrictive.).

Even if you are flying under the U.S. ultralight regulations, you still are governed by the Feds. They say you can't fly a machine that is too heavy, too fast or that has too much fuel. They won't let you carry a passenger, fly into airport traffic areas, fly after dark or charge money for your flying. And anytime they want to check your machine, you have to let them.

Everybody who flies in the United States operates under FAA regulations of some kind. But if you handle things right at the start, you can fly your gyro for the rest of your life without ever having any reason to see the Feds. To make that happen, it helps to know what they expect from you.

Regulations Affecting Your Gyro

Your machine must either be licensed by the FAA or it must meet the requirements to remain unregistered. For a gyroplane to be licensed, it must have three requirements:

1. **Markings on your gyro** - This includes a federal registration number, the word "Experimental" and a data plate. These have to be in the proper size and position, according to the regulations.

2. **Papers on your machine** - You must have an airworthiness certificate indicating you've passed inspection by an FAA official. To get this, you'll also carry a weight and balance statement on your machine.

3. **Inspections in your logbook** - These indicate that your machine has passed inspection once a year. The inspection can be done by you (with proper authorization from the FAA) or by a licensed A & P mechanic or an approved repair station.

Meeting these requirements is not difficult, and once the aircraft is licensed it's done for life, unless you modify the machine. The whole procedure costs $5.

There are FAA employees who specialize in licensing homebuilt aircraft, and they are used to working with people like you. They will give you help just by contacting your nearest FAA office. If you'd like to read more about it, all the important regulations are explained simply in a book titled How to License a Homebuilt Aircraft, available from the publisher of the book you are now reading. The licensing book shows all the FAA forms and tells you how to proceed with licensing in easy steps.

There's nothing in the federal process to keep you from licensing your gyro. But a lot of people choose not to license their machines for a different reason, and it's a pretty good one: To fly a licensed machine, the pilot must also have a license.

If you don't want to get a pilot's license, your machine will have to meet certain ultralight requirements. This restricts you to small, low-performance aircraft which are capable (theoretically) of being flown without the skills evidenced by a pilot's license.

Originally, the unlicensed aircraft were hang gliders to which an engine was attached. At one time, the FAA announced that so long as these machines were "foot launchable", they would not be regulated. This policy led to some machines that looked more like airplanes than hang gliders. To meet the foot launchable policy, some of these had an opening in the bottom of the cockpit through which it was said the pilot could extend his legs to take off standing up, holding up the airplane.

Eventually, some of these open-floor airplanes grew to nearly 200 pounds of weight, and were foot launched one time for the FAA, in a heavy wind by somebody like an Olympic gold medal wrestler in the lightweight division!

To its credit, the FAA observed that this policy was: 1) ridiculous and 2) successful. They saw that these little aircraft were operating successfully and reasonably safely without any federal help (just as the small early aviation industry did before the FAA and its predecessors existed).

As a result, the ultralight category was established in the early 1980's. For the first time in the history of the FAA, aircraft were allowed to be built and flown without federal intervention, so long as they met certain limits of weight, top speed, fuel capacity and stall speed.

The Hollman Bumblebee,
the first production ultralight gyroplane

At first, most people thought that the ultralight category was just for airplanes, since foot launched rotorcraft had not been practical before. But some enterprising individual gyro pilots read the regulations carefully and discovered they used the word "aircraft", not "airplane". These gyronauts modified their machines to meet the ultralight rules and began flying them. Then, in 1984 Martin Hollman introduced the first gyroplane specifically designed to fly as an ultralight, the Bumblebee. A short time later Dennis Fetters introduced the first Air Command ultralight gyroplane.

The ultralight category and the new machines it engendered opened up gyroplane flying to lots of new people, giving them the opportunity to fly free of any licensing of either the machine or its pilot.

The Commander 447 ultralight gyroplane

Regulations Affecting You, the Pilot

There are two kinds of regulations that affect you: 1) pilot licensing and 2) rules of the road. The licensing regulations affect you if you choose to fly any kind of licensed aircraft. The rules of the road affect you regardless of whether you fly as a licensed pilot or as an ultralight pilot.

Pilot Licensing

Not many people know how easy it is to get a pilot's license to fly a gyroplane. If they did, they might not accept the limitations of flying without a license in an ultralight category aircraft.

There are only two steps (count 'em, 2!) to get you flying as a licensed pilot in a gyroplane: 1) Have a medical examination by an FAA-authorized doctor and 2) Have the back of the medical certificate signed off by a Certified Flight Instructor (CFI). You will then have in your pocket a Student Pilot License which authorizes you to do almost everything in your gyro you would ever want to do. It's really that easy to be a licensed gyro pilot. You are then allowed to fly either a federally-licensed gyroplane or an ultralight.

The beauty of a Student Pilot License is that the limitations that come with it aren't ones that will bother a gyro pilot. You can't carry any passenger (Big deal. Your machine probably has only one seat!) and you can't fly into the big metropolitan airports like O'Hare Field in Chicago (Who'd want to in a gyro?). You do have to get your Student Pilot License revalidated by a CFI every 90 days (That's almost a full summer of flying in most of the United States!), rather than once every other year for a Private Pilot License.

Until the ultralight category came along, most pilots of homebuilt aircraft, whether they were gyros or airplanes, flew with Student Pilot Licenses. Now, even though it's possible to fly without a pilot's license, the student license is still a good alternative to consider.

Pilot No-No's

Most gyroplane pilots don't worry much about the regulations that govern where and how we fly. That's because the things you're not supposed to do are things we naturally avoid. Like flying a gyro into Los Angeles International Airport, for instance. Or carrying passengers, or crop dusting for pay, or flying over crowds. Those are prohibited to both licensed pilots flying experimental aircraft and to unlicensed pilots.

There's not much on this list of forbidden flying that would restrict most of us. Almost everything applies to both licensed and unlicensed pilots. Here's a brief summary of your restrictions:

Gyroplane Pilot No-No's

No	Applies to Licensed or Unlicensed Pilots
~~Carrying passengers~~	Both (but licensed pilots can with a rotorcraft rating)
~~Flying for pay~~	Both
~~Flying over populated areas~~	Both
~~Flying in airport traffic areas or control zones~~	Unlicensed (but can do with FAA permission) Student Pilot (restricted from major airports only)
~~Instrument flying~~	Both (Private Pilots can, with instrument rating)
~~Reckless flying~~	Both
~~Night flying~~	Both (Private Pilots can, with night endorsement)

These limits come from several different FAA regulations. The unlicensed restrictions are spelled out in FAR Part 103, which defines the ultralight category. The licensed restrictions appear in FAR Part 61, which describes pilot licensing, and in FAR Part 91, which describes operating limitations of the experimental category.

Rules of the Road

All pilots, licensed or unlicensed, must follow the "Rules of the Road" described in FAR Part 91. That means that a pilot cannot legally jump into his machine and fly whenever and however he pleases. He needs to know the Part 91 regulations so that he can understand what other pilots are doing and what they expect.

Both Student Pilots and ultralight pilots have the same "rules of the road" for the same reason. But with licensed Student Pilots, an instructor is there to assure that the rules of the road are understood. The FAA intends to keep us from filling the sky with the kind of traffic jams and collisions we sometimes have in our cars on the ground.

Here are the Part 91 rules that are of particular interest to gyroplane pilots:

The pilot in command is responsible for the
   operation of the aircraft and for its safe condition.

Experimental category aircraft:
   May not fly over densely populated areas or in
   congested airways.
   Must advise each passenger that the aircraft is
   experimental.
   May fly VFR (visual flight rules) day only, unless
   otherwise authorized by the FAA.
   Must tell any control towers contacted that the
   aircraft is experimental.

Close flying:
You may not fly close enough to another aircraft to create a hazard of collision.
You may not fly in formation with another aircraft without the consent of the other pilot.

See and avoid: When flying VFR (visual flight rules), the pilot must see and avoid other aircraft.

Right-of-way rules:
   An aircraft in distress has the right-of-way over all other air traffic.
   Balloons, gliders and airships have the right-of-way over rotorcraft and airplanes.
   An aircraft towing or refueling has the right-of-way over all other engine-driven aircraft.

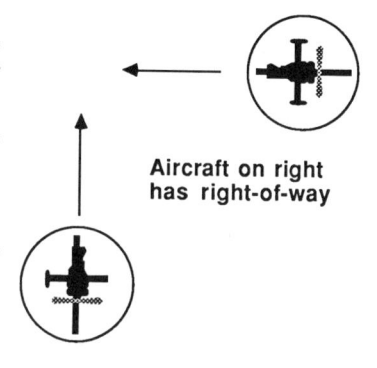

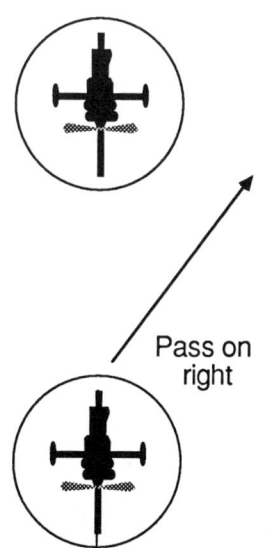

Aircraft on right has right-of-way

   Converging aircraft: The aircraft on the right has the right-of-way, except for the examples above.
   Approaching head-on: Each pilot must alter course to the right.
   Overtaking: The overtaking aircraft must pass to the right. The aircraft being passed has the right-of-way.

Pass on right

   Water operations: When on the water, the rules are similar to the above for converging, approaching head-on and overtaking.

   Acrobatic flight may not be done over any congested area of

57

a city, town or settlement, over any open air assembly of persons, within a control zone or federal airway, below 1500 feet of altitude above the ground, or with less then three miles visibility. Acrobatic flight is "any intentional maneuver involving an abrupt change in an aircraft's attitude, an abnormal attitude, or abnormal acceleration, not necessary to normal flight."

Minimum altitude above ground is 500 feet, except when taking off and landing. You may not fly closer than 500 feet to any person, vessel, vehicle or structure. You must always be high enough to permit an engine-out landing without undue hazard to persons or property on the ground.

Minimum altitude above congested areas of a city, town or settlement or over an open air assembly of persons is 1000 feet above the highest obstacle within a horizontal radius of 2000 feet of the aircraft.

Minimum altitudes for helicopters: Helicopters may operate at less than the above minimums, if this can be done without any hazard to persons or property on the ground. Also, they must comply with routes and altitudes specifically prescribed for helicopters.

Restricted areas: You may not operate an aircraft within restricted areas, except with permission of the controlling agency.

Safety belts: Each person on board must have a safety belt properly secured during takeoff and landing.

At airports with a federally-operated control tower you may only enter the airport traffic area to land or take off. You must be in radio contact with the tower. A helicopter must avoid the flow of fixed-wing traffic.

At airports without a tower airplanes must turn left unless the airport is otherwise marked by lights of markers. A helicopter must avoid the flow of fixed-wing traffic.

Light signals are used by control towers when radio communications are interrupted or when arrangements are made in advance for a non-radio-equipped aircraft to operate at an airport with a tower.

Light Signals

Color and type	Meaning when on ground	Meaning when Flying
Steady green	Cleared for takeoff	Cleared to land
Flashing green	Cleared to taxi	Return for landing
Steady red	Stop	Give way to other aircraft and continue circling
Flashing red	Taxi clear of runway in use	Airport unsafe—Do not land
Flashing white	Return to starting point on airport	Not applicable
Alternating red and green	Exercise extreme caution	Exercise extreme caution

Dropping objects: No object can be dropped from an aircraft that creates a hazard to persons or property.

Alcohol: No one may fly within 8 hours after consumption of any alcoholic beverage. (Some authorities think a greater time interval is needed, but this is the FAA rule.)

Position lights (marker lights on the aircraft) are required from sunset to sunrise. (There are special provisions for Alaska.)

Speed limits: Maximum speed for aircraft is 250 knots 288 mph) when flying under 10,000 feet altitude (lower in airport traffic areas).

Oxygen is required when flying above 12,500 feet.

Chapter 7

Licensed or Ultralight?

Which is better—flying with you and your gyro licensed by the FAA or flying free from federal paperwork in the ultralight category?

The answer isn't as simple as it might seem. There are advantages to either alternative. When you look at them closely, you may discover some advantages you didn't see at first. Flying with a license isn't a whole lot more restrictive or difficult than flying without one. And flying in the ultralight category does not mean you will be free of FAA control.

To help you make the best choice, let's compare licensed flying with ultralight flying. Then you can pick the alternative that seems best to you.

Flying without a license

The ultralight category opened a big door in aviation. Through that door new flyers have entered by the tens of thousands. At its peak, sales of ultralight aircraft were soaring along at a pace of 10,000 new flying machines per year. Most of these took off with people aboard who had never piloted an aircraft before.

Before ultralights, there always seemed to be a wall around aviation, excluding all but the elite few who had the price of admission. It took money—lots of it—and time and willingness to study and learn a lot of academic information needed to pilot the fairly complicated aircraft that were available up to that time. Less than three tenths of a percent of the U.S. population were on the inside, having pilot licenses.

But ultralights were cheap. They were simple. They didn't require any heavy book learning or written tests. They could be flown without a license, and that made all the difference.

Suddenly, through that open door in the wall around aviation poured all the frustrated would-be flyers who had ever said to themselves, "I'd love to fly, but..." It was a stampede, as if airplanes had suddenly gone on sale and each had a sign saying, "Buy one—get a pilot license free."

For one brief shining moment we found out just how much people really want to fly. The strength of that desire fooled everybody, including the FAA who authorized the ultralight category, and the manufacturers who found it hopeless to keep up with the demand at its peak.

Over a period of about two or three years, almost everybody who had dreamed of flying got the chance to find out how it feels to have wings. And, as with any new experience, some liked it; some didn't. The ones who didn't went on to other things, like trail bikes, all-terrain vehicles, computer games or stamp collecting. The ones who did like flying started searching for ways to get more out of their new experience. They found bigger and better ultralights, small licensed airplanes, balloons, replica fighter planes and, yes, rotorcraft.

The whirlybirds came late to the ultralight party, but when they did, the new folks quickly took notice. Once the Commander 447 gyroplane was introduced in 1985, there was an ultralight aircraft that was different. It looked different, and its whole method of flight was different. So many of the new ultralight pilots went for this new rotorcraft idea that they put production of this gyro hopelessly behind the demand for more than a year. Eventually, Air Command Manufacturing not only caught up with demand, but extended its manufacturing capacity to include larger engines, a two-passenger version, accessories and other innovations. Other manufacturers also stepped in with ultralight gyros and new models that require licensing. Today the variety of rotorcraft available to choose from is greater than ever before.

Licensed

Ultralight

An unlicensed gyro has to meet certain design restrictions set by the FAA. While these are continually under review and may be updated, the original restrictions were: 1) top speed not

63

over 55 knots (63 mph), 2) empty weight not more than 254 pounds, 3) fuel capacity limited to five U.S. gallons and (This next one is easy, because gyros don't stall), 4) a stall speed not over 24 knots (27 mph).

To meet these restrictions, the performance of an ultralight gyro had to be limited. The main problem was keeping down the top speed, since it was not difficult to build a gyroplane that weighed 254 pounds or less with a five-gallon tank. A number of methods for limiting top speed have been developed:

A small engine reduces power available, also contributing to weight reduction.

Less pitch in the propeller provides less thrust and "climb prop" performance, something like driving in low gear in a car.

A forward stop on the control stick can limit how much pressure can be applied to hold the nose down. Nose down pressure must be increased as speed increases.

More pitch in the rotor blades converts speed into lift, producing more drag. This generally requires that a prerotator be installed, since it is difficult to start high pitched blades by hand.

Each of these solutions has been built into one or more of the ultralight gyros that have been made available. You can get into a lively argument about which methods are better, but the real answer is to see how an individual machine performs.

Depending on how the top speed is controlled, this limitation can give ultralight gyros less margin for error in certain situations than licensed machines with unlimited power. An underpowered ultralight gyro must be flown carefully in low-and-slow flight, since it will not have as much reserve power. For example, in a balked landing the machine may not be able to climb, and may have to land anyway. If airspeed is allowed to get too low while near the ground, the machine may not have enough power to avoid settling to a touchdown. None of these situations bothers a pilot who keeps his airspeed up while flying near the ground, which is considerably more important in a low-powered gyro.

One advantage of ultralight gyros that is the envy of many licensed machine pilots is this: An ultralight gyro can be purchased fully manufactured, or with very little assembly required by the purchaser. Unlike licensed gyros, which must be 51% fabricated by their owners, ultralights can be purchased with any and all construction work done.

Since the manufacturing of ultralight gyroplanes is not regulated, there are no official standards that must be followed by manufacturers. There is no FAA inspection, and they could theoretically be made of unsafe materials. In the past, some dangerously shoddy machines have been offered for sale, even before there was an ultralight category.

In practice, however, the major manufacturers of gyroplanes make the same machines, with modifications, for both unlicensed and licensed use. The ultralight versions don't have to pass FAA inspection, but they probably could. Also, every gyro manufacturer I know of flies his own machine, and that is probably the ultimate method of quality control!

On the negative side, since ultralight gyros are not licensed, they have no automatic right to use tax-supported airports. You can be denied permission to fly your unlicensed machine at any airport, while the licensed machine owner can only be barred from airports that are privately owned.

Another negative is that the five-gallon fuel capacity limits your range on cross-country trips. But with the more fuel-stingy engines now available, this is not such a big problem since you can probably stay aloft for more than an hour, covering 50 miles or more in a hop.

One of the major myths about ultralights is that they are not under FAA control. Wrong. The FAA regulations created the ultralight category, and only aircraft which follow the regs in FAR Part 103 can fly as ultralights. Those regulations are the ones that limit the performance and specs built into your machine. To make sure you are in compliance, the FAA can require you to let them inspect your aircraft. In practice, the Feds are almost always too concerned with other matters to inspect ultralights, but they can, if they choose, exercise this control over you.

Ultralights must also follow nearly the same "rules of the road" that licensed aircraft and pilots must observe. These are the FAR Part 91 regulations that specify things like "Visual Flight Rules" (VFR), which are the regulations for flying by eyeball rather than instruments; the proper procedure for passing other aircraft; airport traffic procedures and the like. Get caught in a violation of one of these and the FAA will come to see you! (You'll find some additional description of these regulations in Chapter 6.)

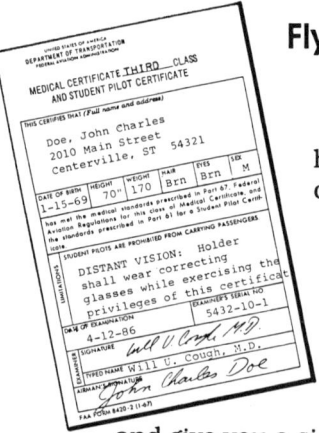

Flying with a license

Would you be willing to pay $100 to have you and your machine fully licensed with the FAA? Surprise! It actually can be done for about that much. Registering your machine costs a mere $5 (There's no charge for the inspection or other FAA services.), while the cost of an FAA doctor's physical can be as low as $50, and the charge to have a flight instructor witness your flying and give you a signoff could be another $50 or less. Add those up and you'll see that the cost of flying with a Student Pilot License is hardly out of reach. Sure, there are limits to the student license (You can't carry passengers; You can't fly into the really big airports; You have to have your license re-signed every 90 days.), but those are not important drawbacks for a gyroplane pilot.

How about all that paperwork? Don't you have to study some dull books and pass a written test for your pilot's license? Surprise! There's no paperwork, no written test and no knowledge requirement for a Student Pilot License, except for knowing the same "rules of the road" (FAR Part 91) that ultralight pilots are also supposed to follow.

But if I license my machine, won't I forever be bugged by FAA inspectors looking at my machine every year? Surprise! You may never again see an FAA person, once your aircraft passes its initial inspection. The FAA ended its policy of annual inspections several years ago. Now, you yourself can be authorized to do the annual inspections of your machine.

Licensed flying does have some drawbacks. If you have one of certain medical conditions that would keep you from passing the FAA medical exam, you have no choice but to fly unlicensed. There are only a few conditions that the FAA won't typically pass (Severe diabetes, epilepsy and major heart problems are examples of generally unacceptable ailments.) So if your body is in good enough shape to hobble into the doctor's office, you'll probably pass the physical.

If you don't like building your gyro, the amount of work you must do to build a licensed aircraft won't sound too good. The FAA says you must fabricate 51% of the machine. That's not nearly as easy as buying an ultralight all ready to fly. But the FAA says it's okay to buy certain critical parts of your aircraft already fabricated, including the rotor blades, the rotor head and the engine. What's left is not too difficult, even for a first time builder.

Another way to acquire a licensed aircraft without doing 51% of the building is to buy a machine that has already passed the licensing requirements for amateur-built experimental aircraft. The FAA doesn't care whether you or another amateur builder did 51% of the fabrication.

This approach has some important cautions, though, if you buy an aircraft already built. One of the biggest difficulties is that you are literally trusting your life to the work of the builder of that aircraft, so that choice has to be made very carefully! Also, since you are not the original builder, you cannot legally make the required annual inspections and must have that done by an A&P mechanic, an FAA-licensed repair station or the original builder. (It would fit the regulations for you to make the annual inspections, then have your work checked by the original builder, who signs the log book.)

Licensed versus Unlicensed

There are advantages and disadvantages to both the licensed and unlicensed approaches to flying. Here is a quick listing of the key things to consider:

Ultralight Gyro	**Licensed Gyro**
Advantages	**Advantages**
No pilot license required	Performance of aircraft is not limited
No federal registration and inspection	Licensed gyros have access to public airports; They may be more acceptable at private airports
No required instruments or construction standards	
No special procedures for buying and selling aircraft	All aircraft will at least meet minimum federal standards for airworthiness
Machine can be purchased completely built or with very little construction required	
Disadvantages	**Disadvantages**
Performance is limited by top speed and fuel capacity	Pilot license is required (may be Student license)
No federal standards of airworthiness	Federal registration and inspection required
Ultralights can be barred from airports	Buying and selling must follow certain procedures
	51% of aircraft must be amateur-built

Chapter 8

Aerodynamic Stability

How do you know whether or not that tail is big enough? Or whether adding a body to a gyroplane will make it impossible to control?

You could build it and find out by test flying it. But that's risky business. It's about like drinking a strange liquid to see if it's poison. No one can predict what a machine will do in the air if it's unstable, but you can be sure you won't want to be aboard to find out!

You need to know, while you're still on the ground, whether or not your gyroplane is aerodynamically stable. If your machine is a proven design, its stability has already been worked out by the designer and you don't have to worry. But if you want to make modifications or add a body enclosure, then you need a way to make sure those changes don't upset the stability of the machine.

An unstable machine can be uncontrollable, with no way to set it down gently once it leaves the ground. It could go completely haywire on takeoff, letting you know immediately it won't fly right. Or it could fool you, acting nice and stable while the engine is blasting air over the rudder, letting you fly around with the throttle open without a hint of its hidden instability. Then, when you throttle back or the engine quits, it could start trying to swap ends, leaving you with no way to maintain control.

It's not hard to measure the stability of your gyroplane. You don't really have to have a computer or go through complicated calculations. In fact, you can do it without any math at all.

What is Aerodynamic Stability?

It's a very fancy-sounding term, but aerodynamic stability really has a simple meaning. It refers to the capability of an aircraft to stay pointed the way it is moving. If an aircraft is stable, it will keep its nose in the front and its tail in the rear as it flies. It will fly like an arrow, not like a tomahawk.

> **To be stable, the center of pressure must be behind the center of gravity.**

The rule is, to be stable, the center of pressure must be behind the center of gravity. The greater the difference, the higher the stability. That's why the Indians stuck feathers on the tails of their arrows: to move the center of pressure back behind the center of gravity. And that's why there are tail feathers on airplanes and gyroplanes, too.

You already know about the center of gravity. That's the balance point of the gyroplane. It's usually somewhere very close to the teeter bolt, or the center point of the rotor blades. The center of pressure is the midpoint of whatever there is for the air to push against. Take the area exposed to the air and find the center of it. That's the center of pressure.

How to Check Aerodynamic Stability

You don't have to hire a Ph.D. consultant or buy $3,000 worth of electronics to compute the stability of your gyroplane. Here's a simple method that uses a five-dollar photograph, a pair of scissors and a ruler. Instead of taking hours of tedious calculations, this system takes only a few minutes. It's easy and it's fun—so much so that once I started doing it I kept checking the stability of several machines just for the enjoyment of doing it!

This method was originally worked out by model rocket builders, who have to be sure their creations don't turn around at launch time and chase them into the weeds. If it works on model rockets it will work on anything else you want to push through the air, including a gyroplane.

Here are the four steps:

1. Take a picture. Shoot a side view photograph of the gyroplane with you in the seat in flying position. Get an enlarged print, the biggest you can, at least a 5" x 7". If you haven't yet built the machine, make an accurate drawing of it from the side.

2. Cut it out. Cut the machine carefully from the enlargement or drawing, giving you an accurate paper copy of the side view of your machine. (Cut out all openings between braces, etc.)

3. Balance the cutout. Put it on the sharp edge of a ruler and hold the ruler parallel to the mast.

4. Find the balance point. If it balances behind the teeter bolt, the machine is stable. The farther back, the more stable.

What you've just done is to compare the center of pressure (CP) and the center of gravity (CG). To find the CP you use the cutout. It represents the area that's exposed to the air, since it's an accurate profile of your machine. Its balance point is the center of pressure.

The cutout does not indicate the center of gravity (CG). That's found only by the hang test. To keep things simple, this method assumes the CG is at the teeter bolt. That's a reasonable shortcut, since gyros usually balance close to their teeter bolts or just in front of them.

How Stable Should a Gyroplane Be?

Let's look at some of the well-designed gyroplanes that have been manufactured and proven in many hours of flying. By looking at their stability we can get an idea of what it takes to have a stable gyro.

A good place to start is the open-frame design pioneered by Bensen. A good example of this type is the KB-2 designed by Ken Brock. Brock repeatedly proved the stability of this machine in front of thousands of airshow watchers by shutting off the engine and making real power-off landings. If it were unstable this would have shown it, since there's no propeller blast over the rudder to keep it straight.

The Brock KB-2 has a center of pressure that is well behind the teeter bolt, about five inches back. It ought to be way back there, since there's not much in front of the teeter bolt to catch the wind. Ken is out there, of course, and that's why the cutout has to include the pilot in flying position, or at least a scale replica drawn in. To get the correct results, you have to treat the pilot as part of the machine.

Having a center of pressure five inches behind the teeter bolt is strong stability. That's why this open-frame design has withstood so many homemade instrument panels, windshields and body enclosures. For over a quarter of a century the Bensen Gyrocopter (which has a very similar profile to the Brock machine) has been abused with all sorts of untested additions, with very few major problems. That naked airframe has its advantages!

A newer open-frame machine is the Air Command gyroplane, which had a similar result. On this machine the center of pressure was measured well behind the teeter bolt, about six inches back. That neatly contoured rudder may look small to some eyes, but it obviously has plenty of area to do its job!

Commander 447

To find out what a body enclosure can do to a gyroplane's stability, let's look at the Vancraft Rotor Lightning. This ultralight gyro has a reasonable amount of added area that surrounds the pilot. It has been flown and proven to be stable. On this machine, the center of pressure falls just behind the teeter bolt—

Vancraft Rotor Lightning

about two inches back. That's enough for it to fly fine in a power-off condition and solidly under power. But it suggests that no one should enlarge the enclosure or put doors on it, since that could move the center of pressure too far forward. That kind of modification should be left to the designer of this machine.

For contrast, let's switch from rear-engine gyros to a front-engine machine. The JE-2 gyroplane designed by Jim Eich checks out to be an extremely stable machine. At first glance it appears to have a rather small rudder, compared to the machines we have just checked. But since there's so much fuselage area at the rear, it all adds up to a center of pressure that is about eight inches back. That should make it quite stable with power off, which may be more necessary in a tractor gyroplane where the propeller blast does not blow right over the rudder.

Eich JE-2

Measuring Stability in Other Directions

With our cutout we've measured stability in terms of yaw or nose-left/nose-right movement. That is typically the kind of stability that is of most concern to people who are designing or modifying their machines.

The stability of a gyroplane can also be measured by the same method from a top view. This will reveal stability in pitch or nose-up/nose-down movement. It will also reveal whether there is a need for a horizontal tail surface. When a body enclosure is added, a horizontal tail surface is usually required to offset the effect of the body. (Note: A horizontal tail surface may also be used for other reasons than aerodynamic stability, such as to affect control response or counteract porpoising, depending on the objectives of the designer.)

Chapter 9

Behind the Power Curve— What's That?

Once in a while you hear gyro pilots talking about being "behind the power curve". This is an impressive piece of jargon, so naturally you'll want to be able to talk about it with the gyro folks. But there are even better reasons to understand it.

For one reason, despite the technical-looking graph from which "power curve" gets its name, it's really a simple concept that you can readily understand once you think it through. For another reason, this is vitally important information. Every gyroplane pilot should understand what it means to be "behind the power curve".

Since a gyroplane can't stall, it is capable of flying behind the power curve without courting the kind of disaster airplane pilots worry about. Some experienced gyro pilots routinely fly in this condition. Airplane pilots never do, except for special training situations. That's why you hear power curve talk about gyros and not much about airplanes.

You can understand this idea easily, even if you don't care for charts and graphs. Very few gyro pilots can accurately draw a power curve, but they should understand these basic principles:

1. Each aircraft has a certain Minimum Power Required (MPR) airspeed.

2. To go faster than MPR it takes more power.

3. To go slower than MPR it also takes more power.

If this seems a bit confusing to you, you've come to the right place. You're ready to look at a gyroplane power curve. Here it is:

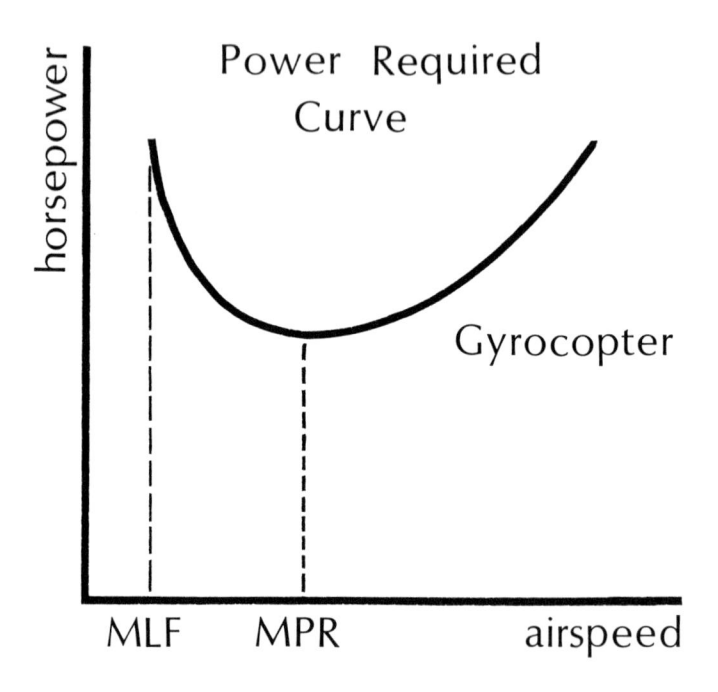

Power Required Curve

(horsepower vs airspeed, U-shaped curve labeled "Gyrocopter", with vertical dashed lines at MLF and MPR on the airspeed axis)

This power curve should more accurately be called a Power Required Curve. It describes how much horsepower is needed for a typical gyroplane to fly at various speeds.

Notice that the bottom of the curve is shaped something like the letter U. At the bottom of the U is a point labeled MPR for the Minimum Power Required speed. This is about 45 mph for a Bensen gyrocopter and for many other similar gyroplanes. At this speed you use less throttle, or horsepower, than at any other speed while you're flying straight and level. (You should also know that this is also the Best Rate of Climb Speed, at which you'll gain altitude fastest when you're climbing.)

Now suppose you want to go faster than 45 mph. You open the throttle, naturally. As you apply more power, the curve rises. But since you're also going faster and faster, it also moves to the right, curving upward. Eventually you're at full throttle—100% power—and the gyro is going as fast as it will go in straight and level flight. That's the top right tip of the U-shaped Power Required Curve. The speed will be around 70 to 80 mph, depending on the power of your engine.

So far this all seems logical, since it matches our experience with cars and other ground vehicles. **To go *faster* than MPR it takes *more* power.**

Now let's go back to the MPR point, with the gyro flying straight and level at 45 mph. But this time let's try going *slower*. How do we accomplish this? We reduce power and begin to lose altitude. But since we want to maintain altitude, we nudge a bit of UP stick and add power to keep from sinking (Remember, the stick controls airspeed.). We're now flying straight and level at *less* than 45 mph and using *more* power. If we slow down further, we add more power (and more UP stick). Now you understand the idea, **To go *slower* than MPR it takes *more* power.**

As you go slower the curve moves to the left, and since you add more power it moves up, forming the left or "back side" of the curve.

You've now completed the whole U-shaped Power Required Curve, with the MPR in the middle and the two higher-powered sides curving up and away from it. Now take one more look at the curve, because it's time for a quiz:

Question 1:   Why is 50 mph a good cruising speed for a gyro?

Question 2:   What happens at the left tip of the curve at full power and lowest speed?

Question 3:   What does it mean to be "behind the power curve"?

77

Since this is an open-book quiz, here is an answer to Question 1: The advantage of 50 miles per hour as a cruising speed can be seen on the Power Required Curve. Fifty miles per hour places you 5 mph above the MPR point, and 5 mph above the point where you begin to fly on the "back side" of the power curve. Sure, the gyro will fly considerably faster or slower, but 50 mph is a very comfortable speed and power setting when you're learning. It also allows for a margin of error in the gyro's airspeed indicator.

Now for Question 2. The "back side" or left side of the power curve is an unstable situation. At slower speeds it requires continuous manipulation of the throttle as the machine tends to speed up or slow down away from constant airspeed. This characteristic is common to all aircraft, including airplanes. As a result, pilots are usually advised to avoid flying on the back side of the power curve. An airplane pilot who ignores this advice is flirting with disaster, since the airplane's stall speed is not far below MPR. At stall speed the airplane simply stops flying and falls until it regains flying speed. The pilot has very little control in a stall.

But what about the gyro pilot who flies on the back side of the power curve? His situation is quite different. No matter how slowly the gyro is flying, its rotor blades are still going several hundred miles per hour at the tips. So the gyro pilot retains full control at all speeds and there is no risk of a stall.

Perhaps you've seen a gyroplane go by in slow flight, its engine revved up to maintain altitude. It is intentionally flying on the back side of the power curve, in full control and in no danger of stalling.

Then suppose this same gyro flew slower and slower until it went completely off the power curve, where not even full power could maintain level flight. This would be slower than 15-20 mph, which is the Minimum Level Flight (MLF) speed, shown on the left tip of the curve. We are now about to see the answer to Question 3, since this machine is now solidly behind the power curve. Here's what happens:

1. The gyroplane will not stall.

2. The pilot retains control at all airspeeds.

3. The machine will begin to settle and lose altitude when it is behind the power curve.

You can sometimes see an experienced pilot flying his gyroplane at zero airspeed, doing a vertical descent. The pilot has full control, sometimes even turning his machine in different directions as he comes down. At a safe height above the ground he applies power, lowers the nose to gain airspeed, and flies away.

There are two things that make this demonstration possible: 1) The pilot is experienced enough to handle this advanced maneuver and 2) He never gets behind the power curve too near the ground. As long as he has altitude below him he can recover and keep flying. But he knows that any time he is behind the power curve he will lose altitude or airspeed or both.

Once in a while you will see someone with a high-powered gyro fly at low speed down to the ground and land. Usually, that's done when there's enough wind to keep the airspeed up even though the ground speed is low. So it looks like the machine is flying more slowly than it really is. But there are some machines that are so highly powered they almost never get behind the power curve, and can actually fly away from a near-zero speed near landing. Or, with high power and a top notch pilot, they can stay only a little bit behind the power curve, settling to the ground at a very slow rate.

Leave the very low and very slow flying to the top pilots with muscular machines. For the rest of us, it's a good rule to avoid the whole back side of the power curve by maintaining an airspeed of 45 mph or more. But if you do fly slowly, make sure it's done intentionally and with enough altitude to be able to drop the nose and regain climbing speed of 45 mph or more. (Another way to practice slow flight is a few feet above the runway. Then if you can't maintain altitude you can flare to a landing.)

Flying on the back side of the power curve leaves less margin for error. For example, if you bank to turn, more power is required and the whole power curve changes. In a 60° bank, easily done by a good gyro pilot, it takes twice the power to stay level. Since that much power is generally not available from the engines we use, you must either: a) give up airspeed to maintain altitude, b) give up altitude to maintain airspeed or c) give up both altitude and airspeed. When flying near the ground, this obviously requires sharp piloting skill and high confidence in your engine. It is a situation to be avoided by all but highly experienced gyroplane pilots.

With more altitude the whole situation is less critical. Altitude—along with piloting skill—gives you room to spare and power to spare.

Here's a word of caution: Slow flight, and exceptionally slow flight such as vertical descents, are definitely advanced maneuvers. There is not enough information in this book to allow you to try any advanced flying. Advanced flying requires more than information; it takes experience—enough to build solid flying skill and confidence.

It is a wonderful enough experience to fly a gyroplane at 50 mph, in a cockpit without limits and with the world at your feet. You are swept along in the machine Igor Bensen called his Flying Chariot, riding on the wind, sailing through the sky. With enough airspeed and with power to spare you can fly back home, land and impress everyone with your knowledge of what it means to avoid being "behind the power curve".

Chapter 10
Beating PIO and Other Nasty Habits of the Gyroplane

There's something about a gyroplane that scares people. Maybe it's the way it looks, with its rotor blades tilted back at an odd angle and its engine roaring off by itself at one end of the machine. Maybe it's the idea of flying on rotor blades without wings; Those rotor blades seem to disappear when they spin, leaving the gyro without any visible means of support. Or perhaps it's the idea of a free-wheeling rotor; It doesn't seem to have any reason to keep spinning.

Some people look at a gyro and shake their heads, saying, "That thing looks dangerous!" Others investigate and discover that the gyroplane can be as safe as any other type of aircraft—in some ways even safer than others.

But even the most dedicated gyronaut is likely to hesitate when he/she hears about PIO. "Pilot induced oscillation"—also called "porpoising"—is a scary thing. According to the talk, it causes gyros to suddenly break up in the air and fall out of the sky. It sounds about as dangerous as anything could be: It kills people!

When wives, children or sweethearts are around, people avoid this subject completely. It's as if it's all too scary for gentle souls—as if they'd never let you fly a gyro again if they ever found out!

81

There are some very nasty horror stories, tales of machines suddenly disintegrating high in the air, leaving their occupants to tumble in terror to the ground and sudden death. In some of these stories the pilots were young and innocent; in others they were experienced enough to know better. In some stories the machines had questionable construction; in others the gyros were showpieces.

Stories like this have frightened many a wife or sweetheart, causing her to turn against her enthusiastic gyronaut. The stories have also scared a lot of pilots, both prospective and active, and have led more than a few of them to stay on the ground.

What should you do about it?

There's something in the personality of many of us that makes us obstinate. In the face of a challenge, we get more determined. We think, "I'm not going to let fear get in my way." We want to grit our teeth and go out there and fly anyway.

That kind of determination is an admirable trait in most things you'll do in life, but it's definitely the wrong way to handle this situation. You can't deal with PIO with determination. Courage won't help you in the least. This is one time when it's wise to listen to that little voice in your head that says, "Self, what you've heard is really scary. You'd better not fly until you check this situation out!"

If you're afraid of PIO or anything else about a gyroplane, don't fly one. Instead, start finding out about it. Knowledge can save you. Acting on that knowledge can solve the problem. And solving the problem can take away your fear.

Can we talk?

I'm going to give you some straight talk about PIO and other nasty habits of the gyroplane. I'll share with you the best knowledge we have about this problem and tell you how people have handled it. The first thing I'll do is describe the problem and help you understand what's going on. This part is going to sound really bad! You'll probably begin to wonder whether gyroplanes are too dangerous for any but the best of pilots. But if you stick around for the other part, you'll read about several remedies that are very effective. By handling this problem right, you needn't be a super pilot, and you won't have to worry about PIO.

Here's the first bit of straight talk: Those horror stories are true! Yes, people have fallen out of the sky due to the problems I mentioned. I'm sure some of the stories have been exaggerated, but, in fact, this is a potentially lethal situation. It can kill you.

If it hasn't occurred to you that you can be killed by a machine that can carry you a thousand feet up and go a mile a minute, you haven't been paying attention. Like an automobile, a gyroplane is a powerful vehicle. Like an automobile, it must be handled carefully.

But here's the other side of the straight talk: PIO is not a mysterious, unknown phenomenon. People have been working on this problem for a long time, at least since the development of the Bensen Gyrocopter in the 1950's. We now understand this problem very well and have solutions that are effective. For people with the solutions, the problem is not a realistic consideration and they don't worry about it.

You could be one of the people who understands PIO, who uses effective solutions to eliminate this problem from your concern. You don't have to worry your friends and family about your suddenly falling out of the sky. Like an automobile, your gyroplane can give you a safe and enjoyable ride if it's handled right.

What's the problem?

It seems that every type of aircraft has an "Achilles' Heel," a fault that's part of the design of the aircraft and that can have deadly results. In an airplane that fault is the stall. If not handled properly, an airplane can stall and suddenly fall from the sky. Many people have been killed by stalling airplanes. Yet, when handled properly, airplane pilots successfully prevent stalling and don't consider it to be a problem.

While gyroplanes won't stall, they do have a characteristic that can be as deadly: the capability to get into PIO. This is an inherent problem which is due to the design of the individual gyroplane.

In some ways the PIO aspect of gyroplanes is like the stall of an airplane. In both types of aircraft, the situations are potentially lethal. In both aircraft, the basic design of the aircraft generates the problem. And in both aircraft, these deadly problems can be avoided by actions of the pilot and by design of the aircraft.

But the two aircraft problems are, in some ways, different. The stall of an airplane is a result of the airplane itself. No matter who's in the pilot's seat, if that airplane slows down to a certain critical speed, it will simply stop flying and will begin to fall. The pilot doesn't create the phenomenon; it's caused by a change in airflow over the wing.

In a gyroplane, the PIO phenomenon gets blamed on the pilot. The "P" in "PIO" is the pilot. It's called "pilot induced oscillation." The pilot doesn't intend to cause the problem, but he/she makes it happen anyway. The stability characteristics of the gyro are partly responsible, but since the pilot could theoretically compensate for those characteristics, he/she is generally considered to be the cause.

While we're comparing airplanes and gyroplanes, I should point out that PIO is possible in an airplane. However, the design of airplanes makes PIO easier to deal with, since airplanes are stabilized differently in flight. Airplanes usually aren't as quick-acting in pitch as most gyros, allowing the pilot time to keep up with the movement of the aircraft. Airplanes fly on wings that don't move; only the air around them changes its flow. Gyroplanes fly on wings that are moving in complex patterns, absorbing energy and returning it in different ways.

One famous airplane that was subject to PIO was the Voyager, which flew non-stop around the world. On takeoff with a full fuel load, the Voyager required constant attention from the senior pilot, Dick Rutan. Dick flew the plane without relief for several days until enough fuel had burned off to make it stable enough to hand over to his co-pilot.

Why don't designers test their gyros for PIO and design it out?

Unfortunately, testing for PIO isn't possible for most gyroplane designers. Without some enormously expensive testing technique yet to be devised, there's no way to fly a gyroplane into PIO to check out solutions.

Airplanes can be tested for stall/spin characteristics by installing a big parachute and using it if the test pilot isn't able to stop a spin. But nobody has figured out a good way to install a recovery parachute on a gyroplane without fouling those whirling rotor blades. Also, I've never seen a skilled test pilot succeed in intentionally inducing PIO. I've seen them move the stick in an attempt to make the machine porpoise, but the reflexes of the pilot prevent the movements that support PIO.

So instead of testing their designs for PIO in advance and then building the final model, gyroplane designers have built their machines based on a theory of what would work, then observed whether there are incidents of PIO. It's a slower process, but it has been going on since the 1950's, and by now the results are impressive.

What's PIO?

"PIO" and "porpoising" are different terms for the same thing. More technically-oriented people say "PIO," while most people simply call it "porpoising" because that word seems to describe the movement of the machine in the air. It's somewhat like the up-and-down play of a porpoise in the water. In PIO (porpoising), the machine begins the fly nose up, then nose down, then nose up even higher, then nose down even lower, and the cycle continues to increase until something stops it—either a corrective action by the pilot or a sudden destruction of the aircraft.

In that worst case, the machine can be tossed forcefully forward. The rotor blades can't tilt forward that fast, so they strike some part of the aircraft—generally the propeller or the tail. This causes a sudden destruction of the machine, which tumbles to the ground.

Some people say that porpoising generally involves three ever-increasing up-and-down swings, with disaster striking on the third one. In reality, there may be more or less than three strikes before you're out.

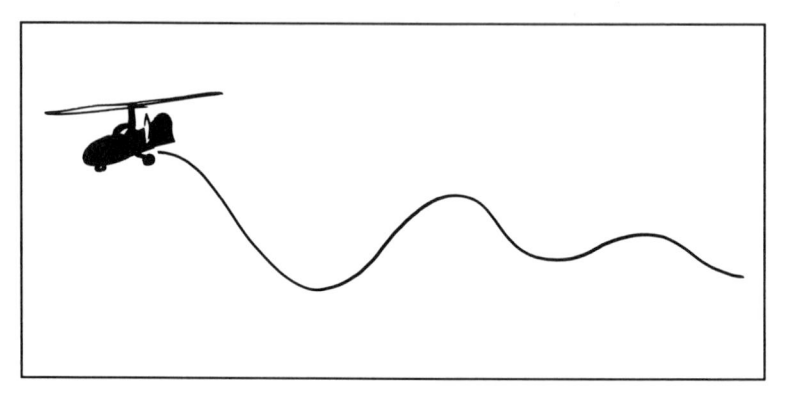

How can this be caused by the pilot? The expanding up-and-down swings are the result of the pilot's movement of the control stick. The first upward or downward swing of the nose may be the result of a gust of wind, a random movement of the stick or something else. To correct, the pilot moves the stick in the opposite direction. But because of forces within the rotor system and the fact that the gyroplane hangs from its rotors like a pendulum, the machine is already building up energy for the next swing, and the pilot's stick movement merely adds to that energy. With energy increased, the machine swings even higher (and lower), and the pilot tries even harder to correct. This further adds to the energy and the machine is soon rising and falling in spite of the pilot's frantic efforts—and, in fact, because of them.

What does PIO feel like?

I can give you a very realistic description of how PIO feels, since I've experienced PIO in two different gyroplanes. The first time was during my early hours of flying. It happened as I was making a turn at about 100 feet altitude on a day with mild gusts. The nose appeared to come up all by itself, as if a strong gust had pushed it up hard. It then went down, just as hard, and came back up even higher. It felt as if the machine was doing this by itself. I certainly didn't want it to do this, and I thought I had enough flying experience not to do a stupid thing like induce PIO. But there it was, rising and falling in ever-increasing waves!

The second time was years later, in a two-seat machine which was completely open with no horizontal visual reference. After we had climbed to about 200 feet, the pilot gave me the stick. Soon the nose began to move up, then down, in ways I hadn't intended it to do. Again it felt as if the machine was doing this, not me. [The reason for this PIO incident after I had many hours of experience was that I was in an unfamiliar gyro with a very different control and rotor system.]

The fact that I'm here to tell you this is good evidence that PIO can be handled. In the first case, the PIO was severe but was handled by a technique that I had read about in a book like this. The second time, the experienced pilot beside me simply nudged the stick enough to calm the machine down. I'll tell you more about how to stop PIO later.

What's the real problem here?

It's not PIO that kills you, it's the sudden thrust forward that does you in. PIO is really just a wild ride that you might enjoy at Disney World if it weren't so deadly. But when the up-and-down movements of PIO get so big that the machine unloads the rotor blades and tilts forward, that's when the destruction of the aircraft begins.

So the real danger in PIO is something else: the "power pushover," also described as "bunting over" or "nosing over."

What's a power pushover?

In a power pushover the machine suddenly noses over forward, reversing the air pressure from the bottom of the blades to the top. This reverse airflow is so sudden and violent that it can produce a loud "bang," as has been reported by some eyewitnesses to PIO accidents. A power pushover can happen not only as a result of PIO, but also in certain other unusual flight situations: high-speed flight and wind shear.

How sudden is a power pushover? Let's ask Chuck Beaty, a highly inventive rotorcraft enthusiast who has built several original gyroplanes and helicopters and served for many years as a technical expert for the Popular Rotorcraft Association. According to Chuck Beaty, a typical Bensen-type gyro could invert as quickly as in $\frac{6}{10}$ second!

Chuck has done a great amount of study of the power pushover and has done calculations of its effects. He explains that it results from losing "rotor thrust." In essence, the rotor blades are no longer pulling upward on the machine, so it's free to respond to the other forces that are applied to it.

Chuck draws a diagram to illustrate what happens. Many homebuilt machines are designed so the engine thrust is higher than the center of gravity and the center of fuselage drag. This is no problem as long as the machine is hanging from the rotor blades in a positive G situation. The pull of the rotor blades (rotor thrust) overpowers the tendency of the engine thrust to push the gyro over. No problem.

But if the rotor thrust is taken away, the engine can push the gyro over in a frontward direction. There's no resistance of the rotor blades to prevent it.

If you'd like to get the feel of this, pick up a pencil and hold it lightly between your fingers. Then, with your other hand, simply push the pencil at a point above where you're holding it. The pencil immediately tilts over, as shown on page 90.

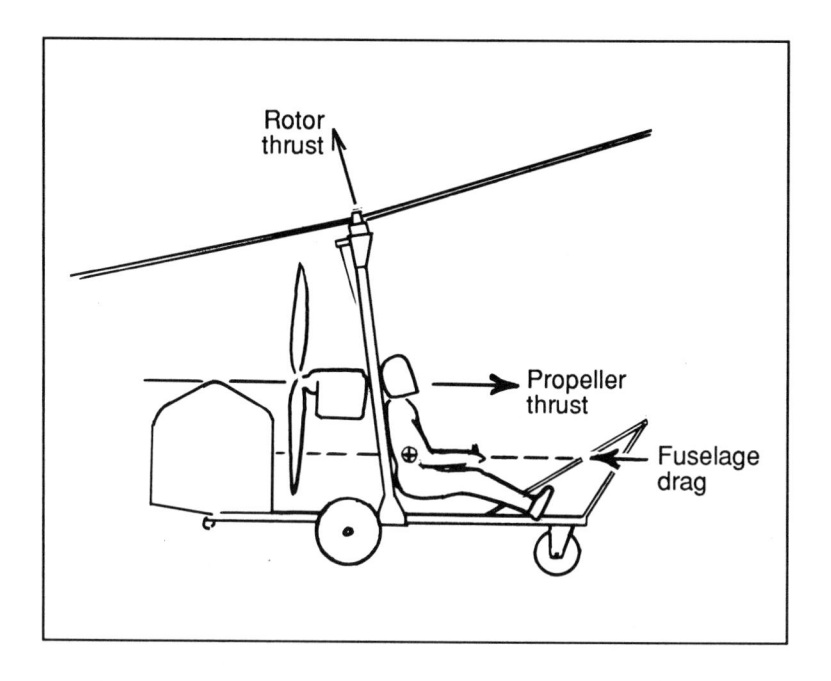

Diagram labels: Rotor thrust, Propeller thrust, Fuselage drag

The point where you're holding the pencil represents the center of gravity and center of fuselage drag. The point where you're pushing it represents engine thrust. And the movement of the pencil matches what happens in a power pushover.

Note that if you have someone else hold the top of the pencil, it won't tilt. That's what you have in normal flight, with rotor thrust at the top of the machine stabilizing the machine.

To make sure you understand the terms, I'll explain that center of gravity is the point at which the machine would balance if it were hung with its nose pointing straight up and with the pilot, fuel and everything in place. It's the top-to-bottom center point of the weight of the machine while in flight. Fuselage drag is the resistance made by the machine as it moves through the air. If you found the center point of this resistance top to bottom, that's the center of fuselage drag.

Chuck Beaty has described a power pushover like this:

"Let's say the center of drag—the pilot's body, the seat, the engine, the wheels, the landing gear—all this stuff is below the engine thrust line. The engine is pushing above the point of drag. With this situation, as you unload the rotors, there will be a point where this thing feeds on itself. As the engine begins pushing over, the rotor thrust becomes less, and because the rotor thrust is less, the engine is able to push over harder. This produces a very violent snap.

"This doesn't even have to be the result of porpoising. If you were just flying straight and level fast enough and you bumped the thing over, it would feed on itself and you would go forward.

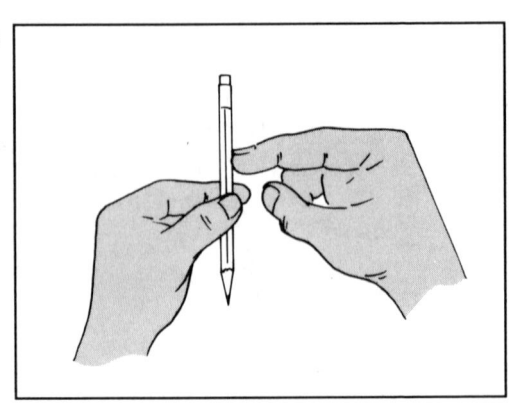

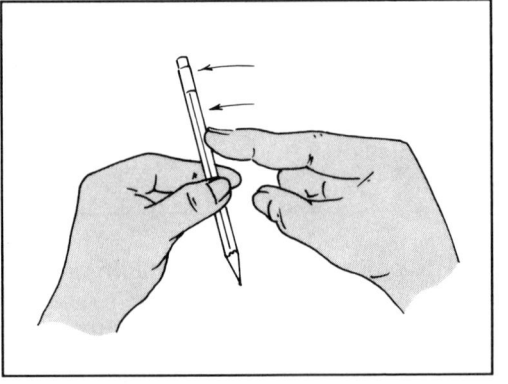

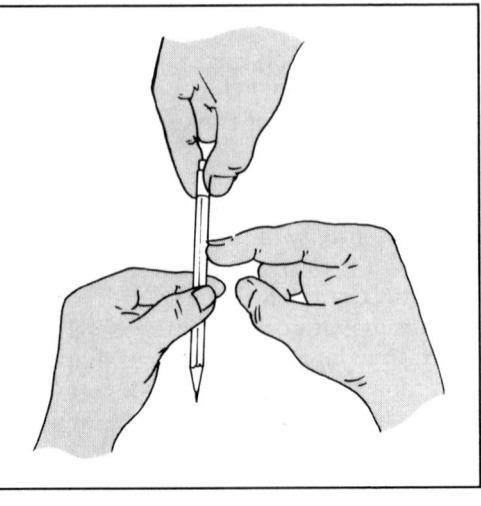

90

"What happens is: The airframe rotates so quickly the rotor can't follow. The rotor actually stalls. On a helicopter you can get into a similar kind of thing where, if you yaw the helicopter too fast, the tail rotor stalls. They call this 'precession stall.' The tail rotor can't precess quickly enough to follow the airframe.

"This can also happen in a gyro. The airframe begins to rotate so quickly the rotor can't follow. The airframe simply runs into the rotor blades."

When is a power pushover not possible?

Fortunately, a power pushover won't happen in a couple of situations: 1) normal flight in a positive G situation, and 2) when you don't have power.

Situation #1 is the world of normal careful people who are competent pilots of their machines. The machine hangs from its rotor blades and the massive pull of those blades keeps the machine under control.

Situation #2 is important: You must have power to have a power pushover. The engine thrust is the motive force here, and if that thrust is taken away the pushover will stop. Chuck Beaty says that if a pilot entering a power pushover could chop the throttle, he/she could stop the pushover. That's more a theoretical possibility, though, since it would take quick action for a pilot to recognize a power pushover beginning, to think of cutting the throttle and to actually shut down the engine—all in less than one second.

When is a power pushover possible?

A power pushover is possible any time there's a significant reduction in the load on the rotor blades (in a machine with mismatched lines of thrust and center of gravity/drag). This doesn't mean it's certain to happen every time there are gusts or movements of the gyro that reduce the blade loading.

Four general situations have been identified as having a high risk of a power pushover: 1) in severe PIO, 2) when flying so as to unload the rotor blades, 3) at high speed, and 4) in severe wind shear. Let's look at these four situations:

1) Severe PIO: In a severe pilot induced oscillation, a power pushover can happen when the gyro makes such a violent upward swing that it tilts forward and suddenly reduces the weight on the rotor blades. With the rotor blades "unloaded," the thrust of the engine can push over the gyro.

2) Unloaded rotors: The pilot can unload the rotors by flying a sharp "over the top" maneuver. Imagine a steep climb in which the pilot suddenly forces the nose down while keeping the power at a high setting. Or imagine that the pilot is flying along straight and level at a high speed and he bumps the nose down suddenly. The rotors could unload and start a power pushover.

3) High speed: High speed increases the risk of a power pushover. You can see this in one of Chuck Beaty's charts. It shows how rotor drag decreases as the gyro speed increases. The faster you go, the less rotor drag. But at the same time, the fuselage drag increases with speed. The faster you go, the more fuselage drag.

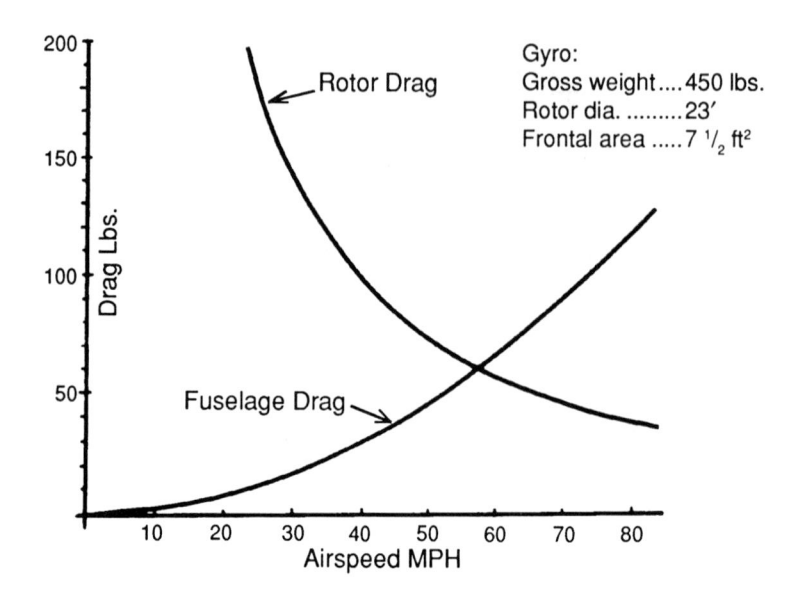

Gyro:
Gross weight....450 lbs.
Rotor dia. ....23'
Frontal area .....7 $1/2$ ft^2

Since fuselage drag is one of the forces that causes the power pushover (along with engine thrust), and since rotor drag is the force that prevents the power pushover, you can see that the faster you go, the greater the forces that produce a power pushover.

4) Severe wind shear: Here we're talking about a strong gust: a strong, sudden updraft or downdraft. This can aggravate conditions for a power pushover. That's because the effect of an updraft or downdraft can be opposite what you'd expect. In a stable aircraft, like most airplanes, when an updraft hits it, the nose moves down. It acts like a weathercock, pointing into the relative wind, which is temporarily coming up at an angle. Likewise, in a downdraft the nose of a stable machine moves up.

But a gyroplane usually has a tendency to make an opposite movement: When hit by an updraft, the nose tends to move up, aggravating the effect. When hit by a downdraft, the nose tends to move down, again aggravating the effect.

Why does this happen? Again, let's turn to a diagram by Chuck Beaty. In it, you see the force vectors acting on a gyroplane that has the engine thrust above the center of gravity and center of fuselage drag. Notice where the rotor thrust meets the fuselage—ahead of the center of gravity and center of drag. This means that a sudden increase in rotor thrust from an updraft will tend to torque the nose up.

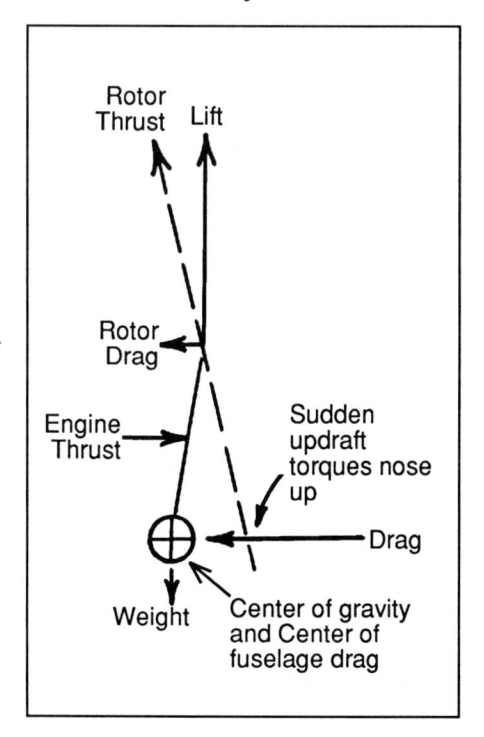

93

Another effect that tends to push the nose up in an updraft is the fact that a rotor is unstable in relation to angle of attack. Chuck Beaty explains:

> "As you go flying along and you encounter an updraft, the advancing blade has more airspeed than the retreating blades does, so the advancing blade develops more lift. In order to compensate for the lift difference, the rotor has to flap more. It's as though the rotor blows back whenever you encounter an updraft so the angle of attack of the rotor increases. This makes the machine nose up more, which exaggerates the effect of the updraft."

What all this means is: Gyroplanes can have a tendency to move the wrong way in the face of an updraft or downdraft. Depending on the design of the gyro and the strength of the wind shear, this can lead to unloading the rotor blades.

Can you demonstrate rotor pitch instability in flight?

Is this merely a theory or does it really happen in flight? In 1990 Roger Wood, an experienced pilot of Bensen-type gyros, tested Chuck Beaty's theories. According to Chuck, if you locked the controls, the gyro would begin an up-and-down course of flight due to the instability of a rotor in regard to angle of attack.

Roger set up straight and level flight in gusty winds at his normal cruise airspeed of about 52 miles per hour (45 knots). The throttle was locked and the rotor head trim was adjusted for hands-off straight and level flight. Here's Roger's report of what happened:

> "First I did not touch the stick when the gyro was hit by a gust. I just let it ride it out to see what would happen. The gusts were very small on the order of five miles per hour or less. I could feel the deceleration when the gust hit. The nose of the gyro would pitch up slightly, the airspeed would begin to drop three to five knots and I could feel a

slight upward acceleration. The nose would gently pitch down and the airspeed would come up.

"The gyro cycled this way two or three times, each one less than the one before and returned to nearly normal flight. I say "nearly" because sometimes the gyro would roll slightly to the right at the first gust. Everything during this hands-off time was gentle and not out of control.

"Next, after setting up exactly the same way, I braced my arm on my leg and held the stick so that it could not move. The throttle was locked as before. This time when a similar gust hit, the nose pitched up more than before, the airspeed fell about two knots more and then the nose pitched down more than before. The oscillations then continued to get worse instead of better. I then took control and straightened everything out. I never let the porpoising get out of hand, but it was my impression that it would continue to get worse.

"Chuck Beaty had told me once that a gyro with locked controls would oscillate this way. I know he was right."

What's the solution to the problem?

By now you should understand there's a problem here that could be very dangerous! I've described the problem of PIO and the power pushover in enough detail to help you understand it. No doubt you're ready for some solutions!

The good news is that there are ways to deal with this problem that are extremely effective. There's a list of things you can do, and the more of these things you have working for you, the less likely you are to get into trouble. Like the stall of an airplane, this PIO/power pushover problem will always be there, and even the most experienced pilot will always be alert to recognize it in case it should happen. But with the solutions available, the problem can be reduced to the point that it isn't a practical consideration.

Solutions involving the pilot

Let's examine four solutions that involve the pilot and can work regardless of what gyroplane design is involved:

       1) Training,

       2) Reduce power,

       3) Keep speed down,

       4) Power before pitch.

Pilot solution 1: Training

The pilot can be the ultimate solution. The highly-PIO-prone Voyager airplane successfully flew non-stop around the world because Dick Rutan had the skill to handle it during those unstable first few days with a heavy fuel load. Some people call Dick the "Velvet Arm" because of his exceptional skill. This is a good example of how a skilled, experienced pilot can deal with the peculiarities of a particular aircraft and compensate for it.

So the first solution is to build pilot proficiency. There's one best way to do this: training. Every new pilot should have training in a two-seat machine by a competent instructor. This will include recognition of PIO and how to handle it. If you're lucky, you may even cause the training gyro to go into PIO. You probably won't consider this a pleasant experience at the time, but you'll be glad you felt for yourself what PIO is like—and you'll be glad it happened when there was an instructor next to you to handle it!

The Popular Rotorcraft Association (PRA) has published a set of safety guidelines, developed by Art Evans, which recommend a minimum of 15 hours of dual instruction before attempting solo flight. The more the better.

Pilot solution 2: Reduce power

Most of these nasty problems you've been reading about can only happen if one thing is present: power. You can't have

PIO when power is off. You can't have a power pushover without power.

Experienced pilots recommend that when you recognize the start of PIO, reduce power. This takes the motive force out of the porpoising movements. I can attest that this works, since it's what I did when I encountered PIO in my early hours of gyro flying (done in the old days when dual powered gyro training didn't exist). Alone and 100 feet up, I reduced power and the nose came down and stayed down. The PIO stopped. I then eased power back in and flew to the nearest landing spot to collect my thoughts.

As Chuck Beaty has pointed out, if you could cut power at the start of a power pushover, the pushover would stop.

Pilot solution 3: Keep your speed down

High speed in a gyroplane creates the condition for several nasty problems, including PIO and a power pushover. At slow speed a gyroplane is docile and insensitive on the controls. As speed increases the control sensitivity increases, getting more and more touchy.

As the graph on page 92 shows, the balance between fuselage drag and rotor thrust gets worse as speed increases, increasing the tendency for a power pushover in a machine with the engine thrust above the center of gravity and center of fuselage drag. Also, the responsiveness of the rotor to wind shear is greater since there's a greater difference in airspeed between the advancing and retreating blades.

Pilot solution 4: Power before pitch

When you change the machine's nose-up or nose-down attitude, change the power before you move the nose up or down with the stick. This avoids the possibility of having a change in power that exaggerates the change in pitch. For example, to come out of a climb, reduce the power first, then if the nose isn't coming down enough, move the stick. This avoids the possibility of the power reduction and stick movement combining to push the nose down too suddenly, possibly unloading the rotor. As a general rule, control altitude with the throttle; control airspeed with the stick.

Solutions involving the aircraft

The machine itself can be designed in ways that can deal effectively with the kind of problem we're describing here. These solutions include:

      1) Horizontal visual reference,

      2) Horizontal tail,

      3) Thrust in line with the center of gravity and the center of drag,

      4) Proper control stick sensitivity.

Aircraft solution 1: Horizontal visual reference

It helps if the pilot can see some part of the gyroplane near the horizon. By comparing that part of the gyro with the horizon, the pilot can have a more critical way to determine how the machine is moving in pitch; that is, nose-up or nose-down. This can be the tow boom of a traditional Bensen Gyrocopter, the enclosure of an Air Command, or some other device. Some builders have simply attached a vertical bar to the nose of their gyros and, at the top of the bar at a point that's near the pilot's view of the horizon, they put a small crossbar. The little crossbar also gives the pilot a reference for banking (roll) movement.

This device doesn't change the handling qualities of the machine. But by seeing the movement of this reference point versus the horizon, the pilot can quickly know how the gyro is moving in pitch and can make accurate corrections with the controls.

A horizontal visual reference is one of the safety guidelines recommended by the Popular Rotorcraft Association.

Aircraft solution 2: Horizontal tail

A horizontal tail makes the gyro more stable in pitch. This makes it less susceptible to PIO or to a power pushover.

A horizontal tail resists and slows down the up-and-down movement of PIO. It tends to reduce the "pendulum effect" of the gyro hanging below the rotor blades. By doing so, it allows the pilot to keep up with the gyro's movement better so he/she isn't so likely to get into a rhythm that reinforces and feeds PIO.

A horizontal tail makes a gyro more stable at higher speeds. People who have added horizontal tails to their gyros have reported that the machines became more comfortable to fly. A horizontal tail seems to offset the tendency of a gyroplane to get more and more sensitive as speed increases. That's because the horizontal tail becomes more and more effective as speed goes up. This corrects for a problem we examined earlier with the graph on page 92. The graph shows how higher speed decreases rotor thrust and increases drag, a condition of increasing instability. But the horizontal tail provides increasing stability to offset this problem.

Pilots have also reported that a horizontal tail makes the machine more comfortable to fly in gusty conditions. The horizontal tail corrects for the instability of the rotor with respect to angle of attack that we discussed earlier. While the rotor tends to pitch up in an updraft, the horizontal tail tends to cause the machine to pitch down. This makes the machine more stable in pitch and helps the pilot deal with gusts.

With all these reasons for a horizontal tail, you might expect that every gyroplane would have one. In fact, for many years most homebuilt gyros did not have them, and many pilots flew without horizontal tails very successfully. The Bensen Gyrocopter had only a small surface directly below the propeller that served as a rock guard during ground handling and added little if anything to the gyro's pitch stability. In the hands of a good pilot who could deal with the quick rhythm of a Gyrocopter's movement, this was no problem. I doubt if Igor Bensen flew with a horizontal tail throughout his entire Gyrocopter career!

You'll find some individuals who don't agree that a horizontal tail is necessary. They may point out that a horizontal tail is an aerodynamic surface that requires forward speed to be effective. That means that at slow speed or in a vertical descent a horizontal tail won't necessarily add to the stability of the rotorcraft. However, since gyros are less sensitive and easier to control at low speeds, this isn't generally considered to be a drawback.

Considering the great improvement in safety you get from a horizontal tail, it's a very desirable component of a gyroplane. It may be the greatest single improvement you can make to deal with the problem of PIO and the power pushover. A horizontal tail is one of the recommendations of the PRA safety guidelines.

What does a horizontal tail look like?

Many approaches have been successful in building horizontal tails for gyroplanes. Some people have made them from sheets of aluminum; others have used slabs of plywood; some have made beautiful contoured tails from composite materials; some have simply taken the rock guard from under the propeller of a Bensen Gyrocopter and mounted it as far back as possible on the tail of the machine. All these approaches can work if the horizontal surface is big enough.

How big should a horizontal tail be? One answer came from Art Evans after PRA had adopted his suggested safety guidelines: Art said a horizontal tail should be "big and ugly!"

Art was emphasizing the point that a horizontal tail should be too big rather than too little. There's no major problem with having too much stability; it's a bit like an arrow with extra large feathers. It's sure to fly straight.

A horizontal tail should be big enough to balance the effect of the rotor and the drag of the airframe. If the airframe is small, the tail doesn't have to be very big. That's one of the reasons the Bensen Gyrocopter could fly without one: It's an open-frame machine without much area to be offset by a horizontal tail. Put an enclosure on a gyro and you increase the need for a horizontal tail. The area of the enclosure in front of the mast needs to be balanced by the horizontal tail.

If you like numbers, there's a formula for the size of horizontal tails that was worked out by the inventor of the autogyro, Juan de la Cierva, and was adopted by later designers of autogyros and helicopters. Cierva established a ratio for the size of the horizontal tail, based on a measure he called "rotor volume." This is the area of the rotor blades (the blades themselves, not the full rotor disk). Cierva's rule of thumb was that the tail area should be about 12 to 15 percent of the rotor volume.

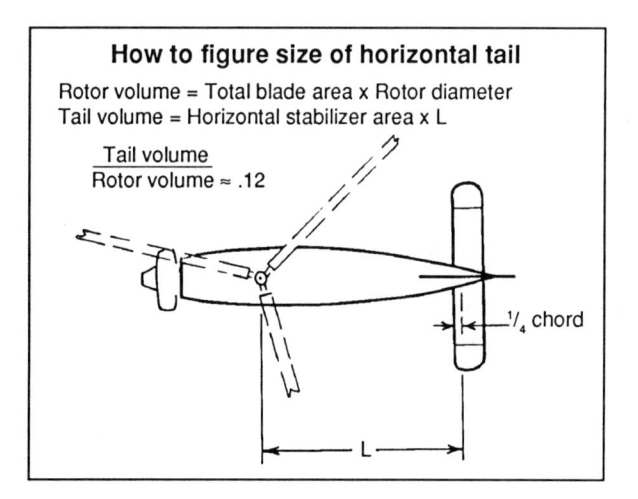

How to figure size of horizontal tail

Rotor volume = Total blade area x Rotor diameter
Tail volume = Horizontal stabilizer area x L

$$\frac{\text{Tail volume}}{\text{Rotor volume}} \approx .12$$

$1/4$ chord

L

If you'd like to know how to figure this, here's Chuck Beaty to tell you:

"If you take the number of square feet in the tail times the moment arm length, that gives a number which is tail volume. The moment arm length is the distance from the center of the rotor to the 1/4-chord point of the tail.

101

"Cierva experimented a lot before he arrived at a tail volume figure of about 12 to 15 percent. Using these numbers, you can't make a gyro bunt over [in a power pushover]. You could unload the rotor for a long period of time and the rotor would eventually stop. You'd fall out of the air, but there would be no such thing as the rotor just going 'bang!' and going over. It's impossible to do that with that big a tail."

Aircraft solution 2: Thrust in line with the center of gravity and center of drag

This is a way to design a gyro to prevent a power pushover. And it's a simple idea.

Remember our pencil illustration? When you held the pencil at one point between two fingers of one hand and pushed on it with the other hand just above that point, the pencil rotated. That was an illustration of how misalignment of thrust and drag can cause a power pushover.

Fixing this problem is so simple you may have figured it out already: Simply push the pencil at the same point where you're holding it. That way there's no rotation.

Since the pencil represents the forces working on a gyroplane, all you'd have to do to wipe out the power pushover is to duplicate your pencil fix on a real rotorcraft. To do that, the gyro must be designed so that the center of gravity and the center of fuselage drag are at the same point as the engine thrust. When this is done, the engine thrust does not make the machine rotate when the rotors are unloaded.

Just in case the pencil illustration seems too simple, I'll also show you a diagram of force vectors, on the opposite page. It was drawn by Chuck Beaty to show his ideal setup for a stable gyroplane design.

When you put aside the diagrams on paper and try to accomplish this perfectly in a real-world gyroplane, it's not so easy. Everything on the gyroplane must be considered, including the weight and size of the pilot of an open-frame

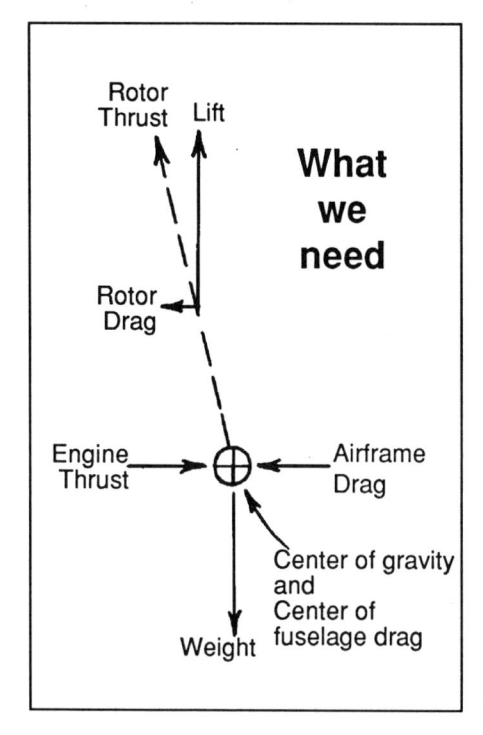

```
        Rotor
        Thrust  Lift
          ↑    ↑
           \   |      What
            \  |      we
             \ |      need
      Rotor _\|
      Drag    \
               \
               |
   Engine      |      Airframe
   Thrust →   ⊕   ←   Drag
              ↑\
              | \ Center of gravity
              |   and
              ↓   Center of
            Weight fuselage drag
```

machine. Since pilots come in all sizes and shapes, one way to keep his/her weight and frontal area in the right position is to raise the pilot's seat so it's centered on the line of thrust. Using a seat tank, with the fuel "wrapped around" the pilot, puts the changing weight of the fuel load on the line of thrust. Designs using this concept have flown successfully and have received reports of excellent stability from their pilots. Note that once the machine is set up with a perfect balance of thrust, weight and drag, any change to the machine can upset this balance, such as a switch from lightweight aluminum rotor blades to heavier plastic blades or vice versa.

Aircraft solution 4: Proper control stick sensitivity

Here's another solution that's part of the PRA safety guidelines. A control stick should not be too sensitive or too insensitive.

Flying with a control stick that's too sensitive can increase the likelihood of PIO. Since the pilot's movements of the stick feed PIO, a sensitive stick can magnify those pilot's movements.

Art Evans worked out the details of the safety recommendations of the Popular Rotorcraft Association. Here they are:

> **PRA Guidelines for Control Stick Sensitivity (Joystick)**
>
> **Fore-and-aft**
> Stick movement should be .800" per 1 degree of rotor head travel. That's the same as 8 inches of stick movement per 10 degrees of rotor head travel, or 12 inches of stick travel per 15 degrees of head travel.
>
> **Side-to-side**
> Stick movement should be .720" of stick movement per 1 degree of rotor head travel. That's approximately 7 1/4 inch of stick movement per 10 degrees of head travel. Compared to the fore-and-aft standards above, side-to-side movement should be 10 to 15 percent less travel per 15 degrees of head movement.

Some gyroplanes use control devices other than a joystick. The overhead stick, connected directly to the rotor head, is used occasionally. As designed for the original Bensen Gyrocopter, the overhead stick is one of the best control devices in terms of sensitivity and feel of the rotor system. Because of this advantage, occasionally people have claimed that an overhead stick eliminates PIO. I can certify from my personal experience that this is not true. My first bout with PIO was while flying with an overhead stick. While I personally prefer the overhead stick, I don't recommend it to new pilots simply because it isn't standard. I don't know of any instructor who teaches with an overhead stick or manufacturer who makes one.

Feel better now?

Now that you've learned about PIO and other nasty habits of the gyroplane, you don't have to worry yourself or your family about this problem. Instead of worrying, you now have your choice of several solutions. You could fly without using any of them and continue worrying. Or you can put as many of these solutions as possible to work for you. You can have every one of these solutions helping to make your gyro flying safer. Isn't that a load off your mind?!

Chapter 11

Thin Air

Getting to know the aviator's best friend

People call it "thin air." You can't see it. You can't touch it. Yet you trust your life to it when you fly.

You count on "thin air" to hold you up and to keep you from crashing to the ground below. You expect it to support your weight and the weight of your flying machine—almost 400 tons, if you happen to be sitting in a 747 airliner.

How can something as light as air hold up something as heavy as a 747? How can air defy common sense and be so durable when it seems like nothing at all? Is there some secret known only to aeronautical engineers that explains it? Is it science? Is it magic?

If you fly, you've probably wondered about the "thin air" that supports the entire field of aviation. Maybe you've heard explanations of lift and how it works to keep you flying. But when you looked straight down from a thousand feet or more, did that explanation give you comfort? Didn't it still seem hard to believe?

Let's find out more about this mysterious substance we fly on and how it works. Let's examine it and find out what really holds us up. Let's put it in terms that will really make us feel better up there, far away from that hard, hard ground.

We don't understand air.

We can't touch air. We can't see it. We can't taste or smell it. If we could, it would probably drive us crazy, since we're constantly swimming around in it very much like goldfish swimming around in an aquarium. Do those goldfish know the water is there? I doubt it. Can the fish see it or taste it or sense what kind of material water is? Hardly. We're just as unaware of the fluid that surrounds us as the goldfish are.

How could you make a goldfish aware of the water around it? Simple. Take it away. Pull a fish out of water and it would instantly start gasping for breath and, in a few minutes, would die. Take the air away from us and you would get a similar result: we would instantly realize something is missing!

Breathing is one way we know the air is there, one way we constantly feel it passing through our noses, entering our lungs and exiting again. Another piece of evidence is hearing, since every sound rides to our ears on the air. Remember the movie ad that said, "In space, no one can hear you scream?" That's true because there's no air in space to carry sound.

Air is also necessary for our sense of smell. Every scent travels through the air to our noses. Yet none of these sensations of the air prepares us to understand what the stuff is really like. In fact, these routine effects of air tend to mislead us, making us think air really is nothing.

Air is not nothing.

There are many misconceptions about air. Our everyday experiences with air confuse us about what it's really like. It seems like a thin, almost non-existent material, weightless and having no substance. There's nothing in our instinctive understanding of air to help us believe that it could ever hold up a 400-ton airliner!

So to understand how we can fly, we have to forget our natural instincts and form a new picture of what air is really like. We need a new concept of the air based on its true nature.

It helps to start by visualizing air as something like the water in an aquarium. Air extends upward from the surface of the earth, forming a big pool. We move around in that pool. Unlike fish, which can float in the water, our bodies are too dense to float in the air. So we walk along the bottom of the pool, typically moving so slowly we can't feel the air around us.

Some of us have managed to make objects that do float in the air the way a fish floats in the water. We've filled big nylon bags with hydrogen or helium or hot air and let them lift us up. Those balloons, blimps and dirigibles float in the air like a fish in the water. They don't fly, they float. They aren't aircraft. They're aerostats. The fact that they can rise up and lift heavy objects (including us) is good evidence that something is indeed filling this big pool above the surface, something substantial that can push really hard!

Balloons and dirigibles show us how hard air can push. But if you want stronger evidence, take a look at the aftermath of a tornado or hurricane. You'll see buildings ripped apart and walls of water lifted to form tidal waves, all accomplished by nothing but air. It's impressive.

But there's even stronger evidence of just how substantial air is: Find a stick of dynamite. Put a fuse in it, put it under a big granite rock, light it and get away! In just a few seconds you'll discover the power of expanding gasses as the dynamite explodes and those expanding gasses tear up that solid granite rock! The expanding gasses of a dynamite explosion are basically the same sort of material as air, even though they have a different chemical composition.

Even from a mile away, those expanding gasses hit your ears and your chest with a "boom!" you can feel. All that mayhem is produced by nothing but "thin air!" Obviously, this stuff does have substance!

A force that can split granite could certainly hold up an aircraft. But day to day, we only feel the mildest possible effects of the force of air—the gentle nudge of a breeze, for instance, or the rippling of our shirts as we race our bicycles down a hill. So we underestimate what this stuff is really like.

Air is a lot like Silly Putty

You've seen Silly Putty, haven't you? It's that gooey stuff that stretches like old chewing gum if you pull it slowly. But it bounces back hard if you form it into a ball and throw it against the floor. Move it slowly and it yields. Move it fast and it resists. Air is a lot like Silly Putty. If you move air slowly it yields. If you try to move it fast, it resists. The molecules of air don't lock together the way the molecules of Silly Putty do, but they do have that same sort of "sometimes soft, sometimes hard" nature.

The things we normally do to air move it very slowly. Walk through it and the air yields so easily you can't feel it. Run through it and it will still yield, although you may be able to feel it a little. Ride a bicycle through it at high speed and you can feel it begin to resist. But in all these actions we're pushing air around fairly slowly and it gets out of our way very easily.

But hit air hard and it hits back hard! When you start trying to move fast through air, it begins to act more like that Silly Putty ball when it strikes the floor. You can feel the air resist at 50 miles per hour as you hold your hand out a car window. The air gets even more resistant if you go 100 mph, or 200 or 500. In fact, at about 720 mph the air gets so hard it forms a "wall of compressibility," the "Sound Barrier" that took so long to conquer. It's strong enough to shatter windows from many miles away as a sonic boom.

To fly, we have to hit the air hard. That's really what we do with our flying machines. We hit air hard enough that it resists and holds us up. We take advantage of its basic nature: air is a lot like Silly Putty.

Producing lift

We have several choices about how to hit the air when we fly. We can hit it moderately hard at 30 miles per hour with a big ultralight airplane wing and the air resists enough to hold the plane up. Or we can get really nasty and hit the air extremely hard at 400 miles per hour with a spinning rotor blade that's only a few inches wide—and there's enough resistance to make us fly.

The harder we hit, the less wing it takes to hold us up. That's why a 20-ton fighter plane can go 1000 miles per hour with a smaller wing than some 30-mile-per-hour ultralights. That's why a 500-mile-per-hour airliner stays up with that seemingly too-small wing.

All flight consists of hitting the air with some object. We call that object an airfoil, since that's the name for any object that gets a useful reaction from the air. An airfoil can be a wing, a rotor blade, a propeller or any other similar object. In every case the airfoil collides with the air; the air resists. That's how we produce lift.

Unfortunately, that simple idea conflicts with the classic explanation of how an airfoil works. If you've heard the classic theory of lift and you accept it, you won't be fully able to grasp the Silly Putty concept of how aircraft fly. Therefore I have to convince you that an airfoil does not "suck" the aircraft up according to the classic theory. It simply hits the air; the air resists.

I don't like the classic theory of lift because it's confusing. This theory has been around since the earliest attempts to explain lift. Apparently it's still accepted in many places that should know better, including some of our universities, engineering texts and even a display at the Air Force Museum in Dayton, Ohio.

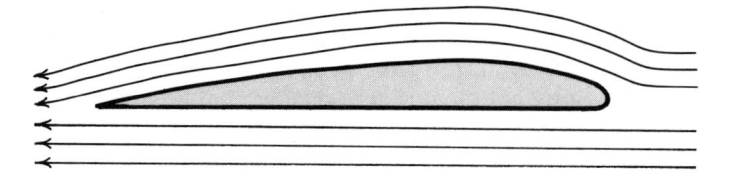

The classic theory says that an airfoil works because air passing over the top of an airplane wing travels farther than the air passing under it. That means the air flowing over the top of the wing must travel faster. According to Bernoulli's Principle, air flowing faster over a surface exerts less pressure on the surface than air flowing slower. Therefore, the air flowing over the top of the wing has less pressure than air flowing under the wing. The wing is therefore drawn toward the lower pressure, producing lift.

This theory is appealing because it's partly true. The air flowing over the top of the wing does go farther and faster and it does exert less pressure on the wing, just as Bernoulli said. But this pressure difference isn't enough to hold up an aircraft. In fact, deflecting the air up over the top of the wing produces a downforce along the leading edge. And the pressure difference between the air passing above the wing and the air passing below the wing is not equal to the lift produced.

To prove the point, you can make an airplane fly without the classic airfoil shape. An airplane can fly with completely flat wings, like a toy glider made from sheet balsa wood or a paper airplane. A flat wing can't work as the classic theory says it does. Something else has to be producing the lift. What is it?

It's this: The wing works by deflecting air downward. The wing drives the air downward and the wing is driven upward. It's the old action-reaction effect that Isaac Newton talked about 200 years ago. If you push air down, the reaction will push you up. If you push enough air and push it hard enough, you will fly.

A very simple example of this effect is a rocket. The exhaust blasts out the tail of the rocket and the reaction drives the rocket upward. Inside the rocket engine, the fuel is turned into gasses that are accelerated out the nozzle with great force. On very large rockets the force can be measured in tons, and very, very heavy payloads can be lifted by that reaction. It can be a big enough blast to send you to the moon!

The wing of an airplane works, in principle, like that rocket engine. But instead of accelerating gas out a nozzle by a chemical reaction, the wing accelerates a gas (air) downward by a mechanical reaction. The wing just deflects the air downward. This action produces the same reaction; the wing is pushed upward.

Then what's the point of a specially-shaped airfoil in an airplane wing? The point is this: The specially-shaped airfoil is a more efficient way to push the air down. The air coming over and under a well-shaped wing is pushed down more effectively. That's why a well-shaped wing produces more lift.

A wing always flies in a position that's slightly tilted up, a bit like a stone skipping over the surface of the water. That upward tilt is called the angle of incidence, and it's a way of deflecting the air downward.

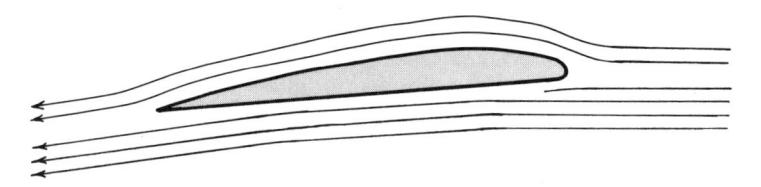

That's why a toy airplane can fly with a flat wing. It has an angle of incidence and deflects the air downward. Unfortunately, as it flies, the flat wing generates turbulence behind its top surface. But if the wing is curved into the shape of a typical airfoil, there's less turbulence and the air is more effectively deflected downward.

Ninety years ago, the Wright brothers' wind tunnel tests showed that certain airfoil shapes produced more lift. Wilbur and Orville didn't know exactly how those shapes worked, but they knew which ones worked best, and that knowledge allowed the Wrights to fly better then anyone else. Over the years, people improved airfoils by the same trial-and-error method used by the Wrights. It didn't matter that people believed Bernoulli's Principle was the only thing keeping airplanes up; the planes would still fly anyway.

Helicopters fly, too

When rotary-wing aircraft were developed, the designers quickly discovered that rotor blades also work better with certain shapes that look a lot like the airplane wing shapes. That's because they have the same purpose, to deflect air downward.

On a helicopter or autogyro, lift is produced the same way, by pushing the air down. A whirling rotor blade does this violently, hitting the air very hard at hundreds of miles per hour. That's why those tiny rotor blades can hold up those big heavy helicopters and autogyros, because they're hitting the air hard and the air is acting solid, like Silly Putty.

But wait! Isn't there something in the textbooks about air flowing downward through helicopter rotors and upward through autogyro rotors? Does this mean autogyros don't fly by pushing air downward?

No. In every case lift comes from deflecting air downward. It's obvious in a helicopter, where the powered rotor disk is tilted forward and aggressively presses the air down. But in the backward-tilted free-wheeling autogyro rotor, it's a bit more difficult to see.

That's because we're visualizing the spinning rotor blade as a disk. The air appears to enter the bottom of the disc and to exit at the top. But the rotor blades are not really a disk; we're just pretending they are. The autogyro rotor blades hit the air and push it down, then they move on. The air left behind them is actually lower than it was before its encounter with the blades.

What is air?

Air is a gas. A mixture of gasses, really. A messy, impure mixture of swirling chemicals. A chemist would tell you it's mainly nitrogen–about 78%–while another 21% is oxygen. That accounts for 99% . The rest of air is mainly argon (.93%) and the balance (.07%) is made up of relatively small amounts of many other gasses, including carbon dioxide. Even though some people get very concerned about the volume of carbon dioxide in the air and its influence on the "Greenhouse Effect," it actually makes up only .03 % of air, or 3/10,000. Many other gasses are also in the air in lesser quantities, and for the purposes of flying, can be ignored.

The Recipe for Air

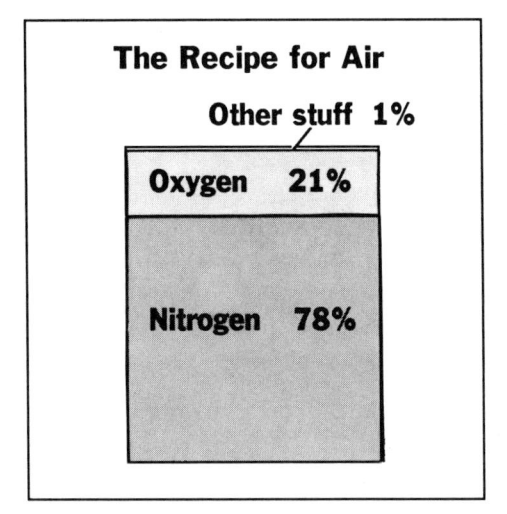

Other stuff 1%
Oxygen 21%
Nitrogen 78%

Mixed into this gas soup called air is some water vapor. That's water that has turned into a gas itself. There may also be trace amounts of the vapor forms of other materials, but water is the main one to know about, since it can change the consistency of the air, making it "thinner" or "thicker."

Lots of water vapor in the air makes the air thinner. Dry air is thicker. That may be the opposite of what you'd expect, since a bucket of water is rather heavy. Also, we talk about "thick" fog when the air is saturated with water vapor (100% relative humidity). But when you see water in a bucket or as fog, you're not seeing water vapor. You're seeing liquid water. In its vapor form, water is completely invisible, and it's lighter than air (Remember, water is mainly hydrogen, the lightest element in the universe, while air is mainly nitrogen, a heavier element).

There's also dirt in the air, little microscopic chunks that float around in it, sometimes called "particulate matter." These can be minuscule pieces of soil that were tossed up by a brisk wind, teensy specks of carbon that came out of a volcano somewhere, or even organic junk that's tossed out by plants or animals. These particles are so small you ordinarily can't see them. But when they get together by the umtillions, especially when each particle gets wrapped in water or ice, they can form a cloud.

So air isn't a neat and consistent material. The air above Kansas City is different from the air above Saskatoon. The air during a rain is different from the air during a drought. The air in the morning is different from the air in the night.

Some of it is thinner, some thicker, some dirtier, some wetter, some has more or less oxygen or other components—and aviators are likely to try to fly in all of it!

Air is substantial stuff

Air is a gas, which doesn't seem very substantial. But if air were liquid, you wouldn't be surprised that it can hold us up. For example, water skiers don't worry about that liquid stuff that supports them. Water is thick, juicy, and you can see it.

Air is more liquid than you think. In fact, the only thing that keeps air from being like water is the fact that air molecules are typically bouncing around, colliding with each other and constantly moving. If they ever slow down, they become a liquid.

That bouncing around of molecules is generally known by another name: "heat." That's what heat is, the kinetic energy of molecules wiggling and bouncing and colliding with other molecules. At the temperatures in which we fly, air has so much kinetic energy that the molecules don't stick together very well and they act as a gas. But get rid of that energy and most components of the air start acting like the water in that goldfish tank.

You've probably seen liquid air, or at least the major components of air in liquid form. Look at nitrogen, for instance (which makes up about 78% of air). Take the heat out of nitrogen and you have liquid nitrogen, the watery, ultra-cold stuff used for storing biological chemicals, superconducting electronic circuits and the like.

Oxygen (which makes up about 21% of air), also becomes a liquid when you take the heat out of it. In liquid form, oxygen is piped into rocket engines as a component of the fuel (It's often called "LOX"). And if you want to see just how solid some of these components of air are, look at carbon dioxide. This stuff is so solid when you take the heat out that you can buy chunks of it to keep your ice cream frozen. You call it "dry ice."

But if you warm up liquid nitrogen and liquid oxygen, with a pinch of dry ice, you have air. In gas form, those elements float around, acting light and ethereal, and we fly on them. Each one of the air molecules that we fly on is just as firm as it would be in liquid or solid form. Each air molecule is just busier bouncing around, full of the kinetic energy we call "heat."

When we fly, we're really skimming along on top of a cushion of fluid called air, just like a water skier. It's simple. It's no worry.

Getting comfortable in the air

You don't have to have that queasy feeling when you're looking down from an aircraft in flight. If you understand the true nature of air, you can overcome the natural instinct that gives us a fear of heights. Even though you usually can't see the air, you'll feel more secure if you know that the air is really there, it's really powerful and it's really acting a lot like Silly Putty.

And if that doesn't work, use the air another way: Take a deep breath!

Chapter 12

Common Gyroplane Terms

It's always nice to be able to speak the language. And gyroplanes, like other special interests, have their own terms. Here's a listing of some of the more technical terms that you are likely to encounter, either in this book or in hanger talk. Each term is explained in non-technical language.

Angle of Attack - The angle at which the air meets the rotor blade.

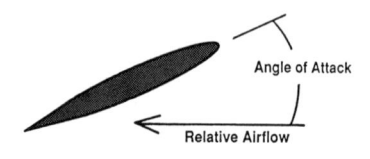

Blade Loading - The gross weight of the gyroplane divided by the total rotor blade area, usually expressed in pounds per square foot.

Center of Gravity - The center point of all the weight of an object. An object would balance at this point.

Center of Pressure - The center point of all the aerodynamic forces on an object.

Chord - An imaginary line drawn through the center of a rotor blade from front to back. This term also refers to the width of a rotor blade from front to back.

Disc Loading - The gross weight of a gyroplane divided by the rotor disc area, usually expressed in pounds per square foot. This rotorcraft term corresponds to "wing loading" in airplanes.

Drag - A reaction to the force of thrust. Drag acts parallel to the relative airflow and opposite the direction of thrust. This term also is sometimes used to describe the lead/lag action of rotor blades.

Force - Any influence which tends to change the state of motion of an object.

Ground Cushion or **Ground Effect** - The compacted air trapped under an aircraft operating near the ground results in increased lift.

Gyroscopic Precession - The tendency of a rapidly rotating object (a gyroscope) to tilt at right angles to a push.

Lift - A result of aerodynamic forces which acts at right angles to the relative airflow.

One per Rev - An abbreviation for a vibration that occurs once during each complete revolution of the rotor blades. In a two-bladed rotor, this is usually an indication of out-of-track or out-of-balance rotors.

Phase Lag - The delay in response of a rotor to a change in pitch. This occurs up to 90° after the change in pitch.

Pitch - The angle between a rotor blade and a reference surface such as the rotor hub. This same term also refers to nose up/nose down movement of an aircraft.

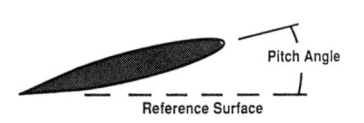

Power Loading - The gross weight of a gyroplane divided by the horsepower of the engine. It is usually expressed in pounds per horsepower.

Reaction - The result of the action of a force. As Isaac Newton said, "For every action there is a reaction which is equal in force and opposite in direction".

Relative Airflow - This refers to the direction and velocity of air moving past a part of an aircraft. Actually, it is not the air that moves but the aircraft. The relative airflow is often visualized as if it were moving past the aircraft, as in a wind tunnel.

Resultant Force - If two or more forces act on an object, the apparent single force that represents the combination of the two is the resultant force.

Rotor Disc - The imaginary circular-shaped area that is formed when the rotor spins.

Root - The end of the rotor blade nearest the hub.

Solidity Ratio - The rotor blade area divided by the rotor disc area.

Tip-Speed Ratio - The ratio between the forward speed of the gyroplane and the rotational speed of the rotor blade tip.

Teeter Bolt - The single bolt on which a semi-rigid rotor pivots. This allows the rotor to teeter or flap. It has sometimes been called the "Jesus bolt".

Two per Rev - An abbreviation for a vibration that occurs two times for each complete revolution of the rotor blades. In a two-bladed rotor it is typically an indication of rotor blade stall or flapping.

Vector - A straight line drawn to represent a force or velocity. The length of the line indicates the magnitude. The direction of the line represents the direction of the force or velocity.

Index

Advancing/retreating blades 25,37,38
Air 105-115
Air composition 113
Angle of attack 81
Autorotation 4,28,30,33,34
Autogyro 13-17,22
Balancing rotor blades 43,48,49
Blade loading 81
Bensen, Igor 18-20
Berliner, Emil 8
Bothezal, George 8
Breguet, Louis 7,8
Caley, George 7
Center of gravity 81, 89
Center of pressure 81
Chinese top 6,7
Chord 81
Cierva, Juan de la 9-13,15-17,24,25,37,40
Contents 1
Control stick sensitivity 103, 104
Cornu, Paul 8
Coriolis force 41
DaVinci, Leonardo 7
Dissymetry of lift 37
Disc loading 81
Downdrafts 93, 94
Drag 81
Edison, Thomas 7
Ellehammer, Jacob 8
FAR Parts 61,91,103 - 56
Feathering 43
Flapping 38
Focke-Achgelis aircraft 17,18
Focke, Henrich 17
Force 82
Ground cushion/effect 82
Gyrocopter 19,20
Gyroplane, origin of name 7,8
Gyroscopic precession 82
Helicopter, origin of name 7
Horizontal tail 99, 100, 101
Horizontal reference 98
Kellett autogyro 16
Launoy and Bienvenu 6
Lead/lag 36,40-42
Licensing, gyroplane 50,51,67,68
  pilot 50,53-60,66-68
Lift 29,30,82, 108, 109
Lilienthal, Otto 8
Oehmichen, Etienne 8
One-per-rev 82
Pescara, Raul 8
Phase lag 82
PIO (pilot induced oscillation) 81-104
PIO aircraft solutions 98-104
PIO pilot solutions 96-98
Pitcairn, Harold 15-18
Pitch 82
Popular Rotorcraft Association (PRA) 20
Power curve 75-80
Power loading 82
Power pushover 87-104
Pre-coning 43
Reaction 82
Relative airflow 82
Resultant force 83
Rotachute 18,19
Rotor disc 83
Rotors, Articulated 43
  Rigid 43
  Semi rigid 39,40,42
Root 83
Rotor pitch instability 94-95
Rotor volume 101, 102
Rules of the road 53-60
Safety guidelines 98, 100, 104
Sikorsky, Igor 17
Skipping stone concept 31,32
Squirting soap concept 32
Stability 69-74
Solidity ratio 83
Teeter bolt 83
Teetering 36,38,39
Tip-speed ratio 83
Tracking rotor blades 43-48
Two-per-rev 83
Updrafts 93, 94
Ultralight aircraft 50,52,53,61-68
Unloading the rotor 91, 92
Universal joint effect 41
Vector 83
Wind shear 93
Wright, Wilbur and Orville 8,9